HORST
HIGHLIGHTS

First published by V&A Publishing, 2014
Victoria and Albert Museum
South Kensington
London SW7 2RL
www.vandapublishing.com

© Victoria and Albert Museum, London

2018 2017 2016 2015 2014
10 9 8 7 6 5 4 3 2 1

ISBN 978 1 85177 816 4

A catalogue record for this book is
available from the British Library.

All photographs by Horst P. Horst.
Images reproduced courtesy of the Condé Nast Archive,
New York, Collection Condé Nast, France, and the Horst Estate.

Front cover: Helen Bennett, Paris 1936
Back cover: Hat by John-Frederic, 1943

Designer: Jevon Hall

Printed in China

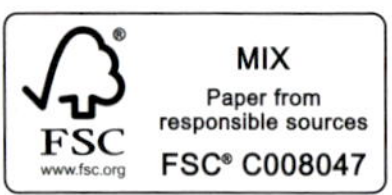

V&A Publishing

Supporting the world's leading
museum of art and design,
the Victoria and Albert
Museum, London

HORST
HIGHLIGHTS

Susanna Brown

V&A Publishing

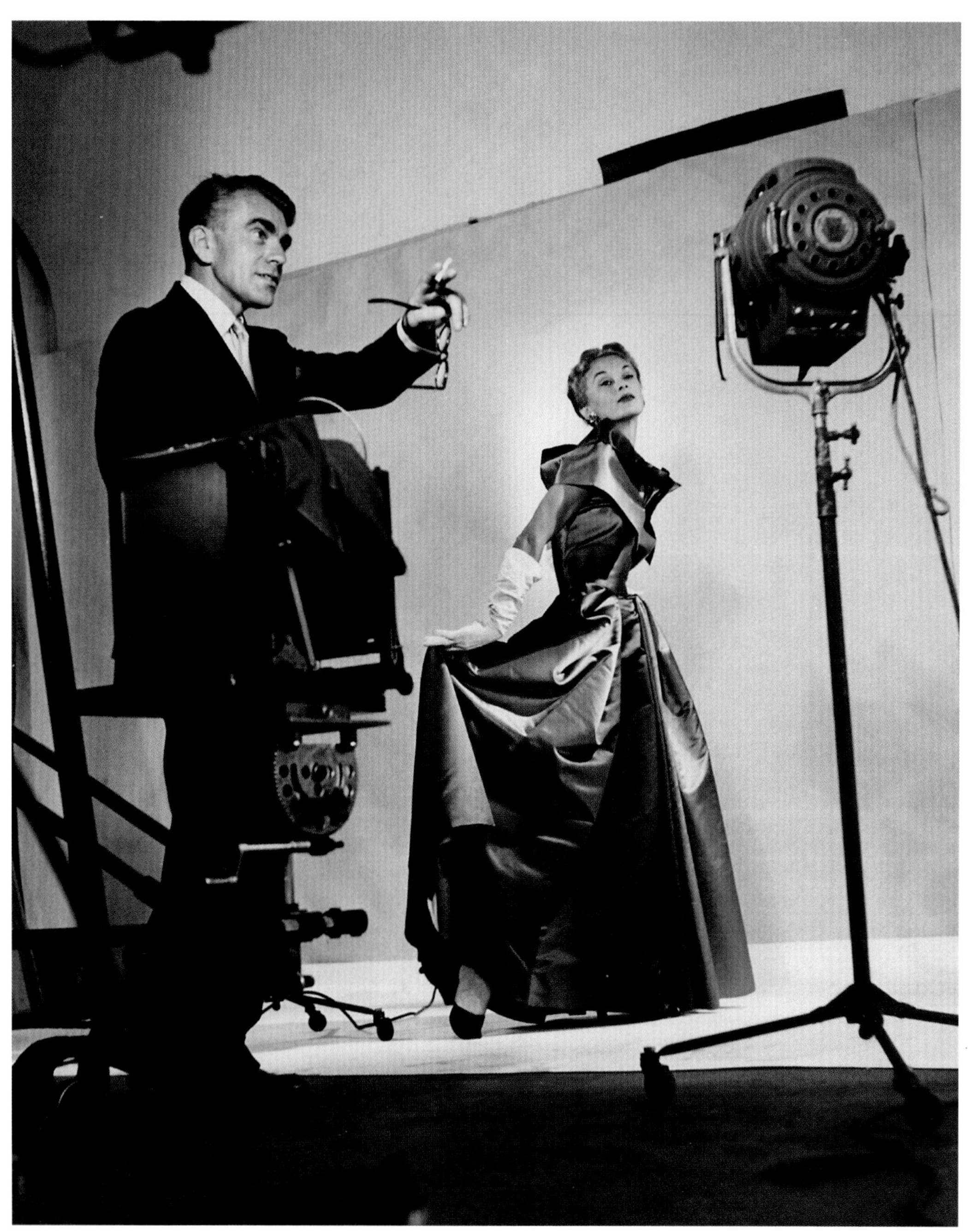

Roy Stevens, Horst and Lisa Fonssagrives in the studio, New York, 1949

"Fashion is an expression of the times. Elegance is something else again."

Horst P. Horst (1906–1999) created images that transcend fashion and time. He was a master of light, composition and atmospheric illusion, who conjured a world of sensual sophistication. In an extraordinary sixty-year career, his photographs graced the pages of *Vogue* and *House and Garden* under the one-word photographic byline 'Horst' and he ranks alongside Irving Penn and Richard Avedon as one of the twentieth century's pre-eminent fashion and portrait photographers.

German-born Horst studied design and construction in Hamburg. In 1930, he moved to Paris, where he befriended Baron George Hoyningen-Huene, one of *Vogue*'s first star photographers, famous for his classically inspired fashion images in which models pose atop columns to resemble caryatids, or lounge in chic beachwear, bathed in light. Horst's relationship with Huene led to lessons with the camera and an opportunity to hone his skills in the photographic studio of French *Vogue*. Horst's first published photographs appeared in *Vogue* in 1931 and by the mid-1930s he had superseded his mentor as Paris *Vogue*'s primary photographer. Horst assimilated Huene's Neoclassical approach and skilfully combined it with elements of Modernism and Baroque, punctuated by surreal and humorous touches. Chiaroscuro effects, spotlighting and dramatic shadows were key elements of Horst's 1930s images. With an instinctive sense of form, he turned simple materials into seemingly luxurious sets.

The 1930s ushered in huge technical advancements in colour photography and Horst possessed a nuanced understanding of chromatic relationships that allowed him to adapt to a new visual vocabulary. He went on to create some of *Vogue*'s most striking colour images, and more than ninety covers for the magazine. In August 1939, just weeks before the outbreak of the Second World War, Horst fled Paris for New York. Horst became an American citizen; he changed his surname from 'Bohrmann' to 'Horst' in 1943 and joined the US Army. After the war, the American fashion industry boomed and Horst was as busy as ever before. His extraordinary range and work outside *Vogue* convey Horst's relentless visual curiosity and life-long desire for new photographic challenges. Personal projects include the detailed exploration of natural forms published as *Patterns from Nature* in 1946, contemplative still life arrangements, and powerful documentary pictures from his international travels. An extensive series exploring some of the world's most magnificent homes and gardens marked a new phase in Horst's career in the 1960s. When the next generation discovered his early black and white studies in the 1970s, Horst was in demand once more and he began to produce exquisite platinum-palladium prints for collectors and museums.

The V&A is home to the oldest museum photography collection in the world. It is designated the UK's National Collection of the Art of Photography and spans the whole history of the medium. This book is published to coincide with the V&A's major exhibition *Horst: Photographer of Style*. The Museum's permanent collection includes more than 30 photographs by Horst, many of which were generously donated to the V&A in 2013 by Gert Elfering, art collector and owner of the Horst Estate.

Horst quoted in Valentine Lawford,
Horst: His Work and His World (New York, 1984), p.392.

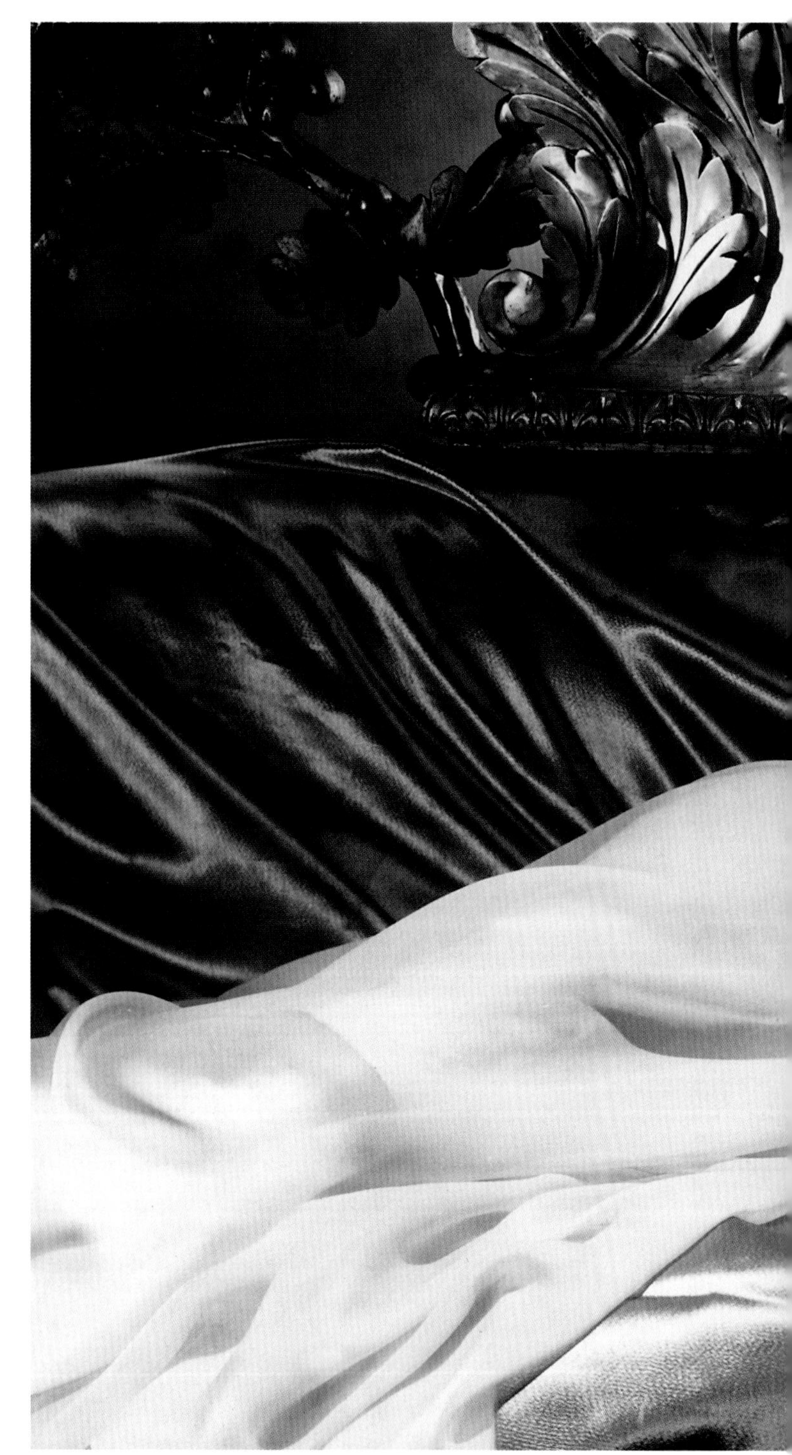

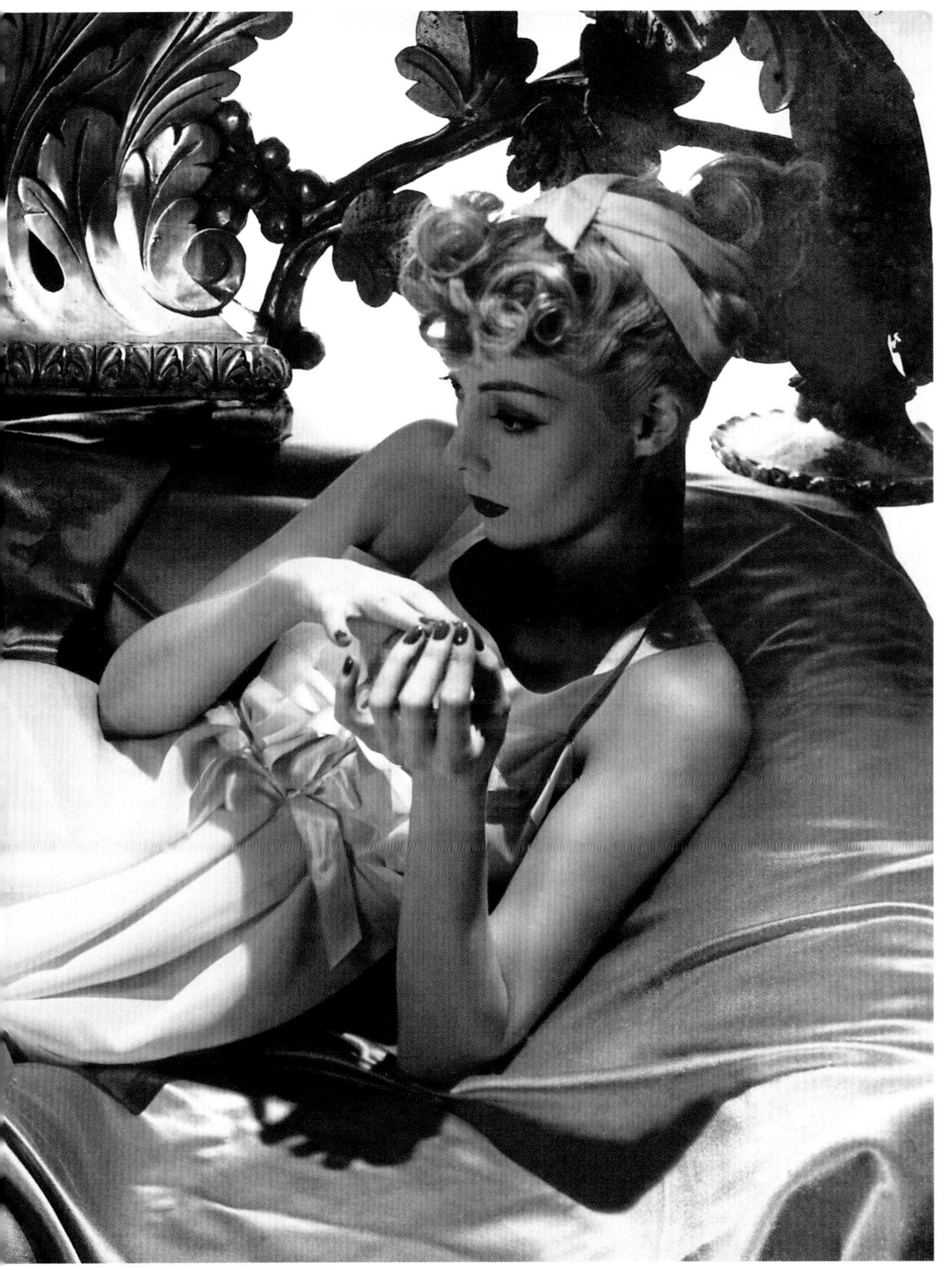

Helen Bennett, *nightgown by Dubrulle, 1938*

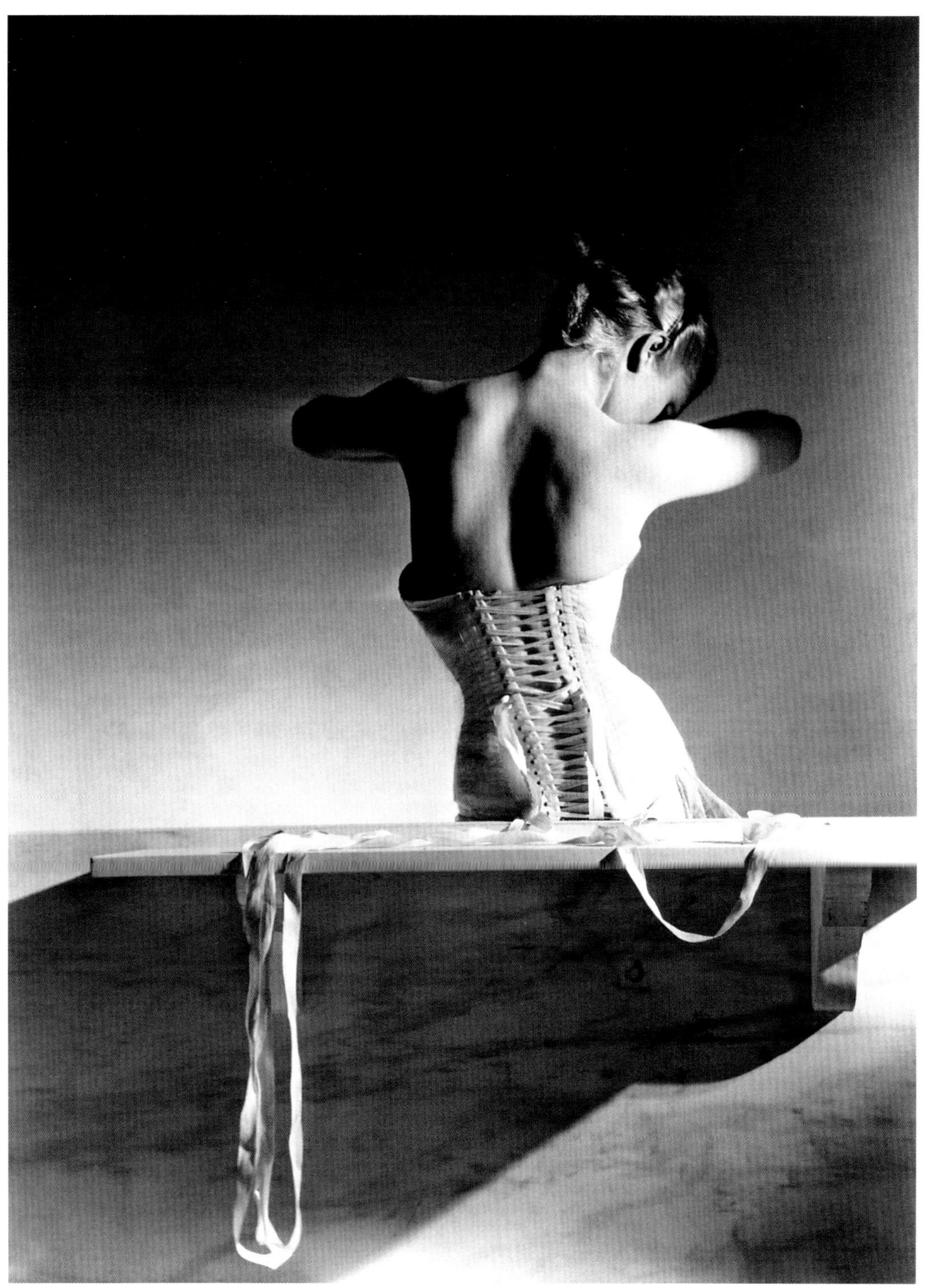

Madame Bernon, corset by Detolle for Mainbocher, 1939

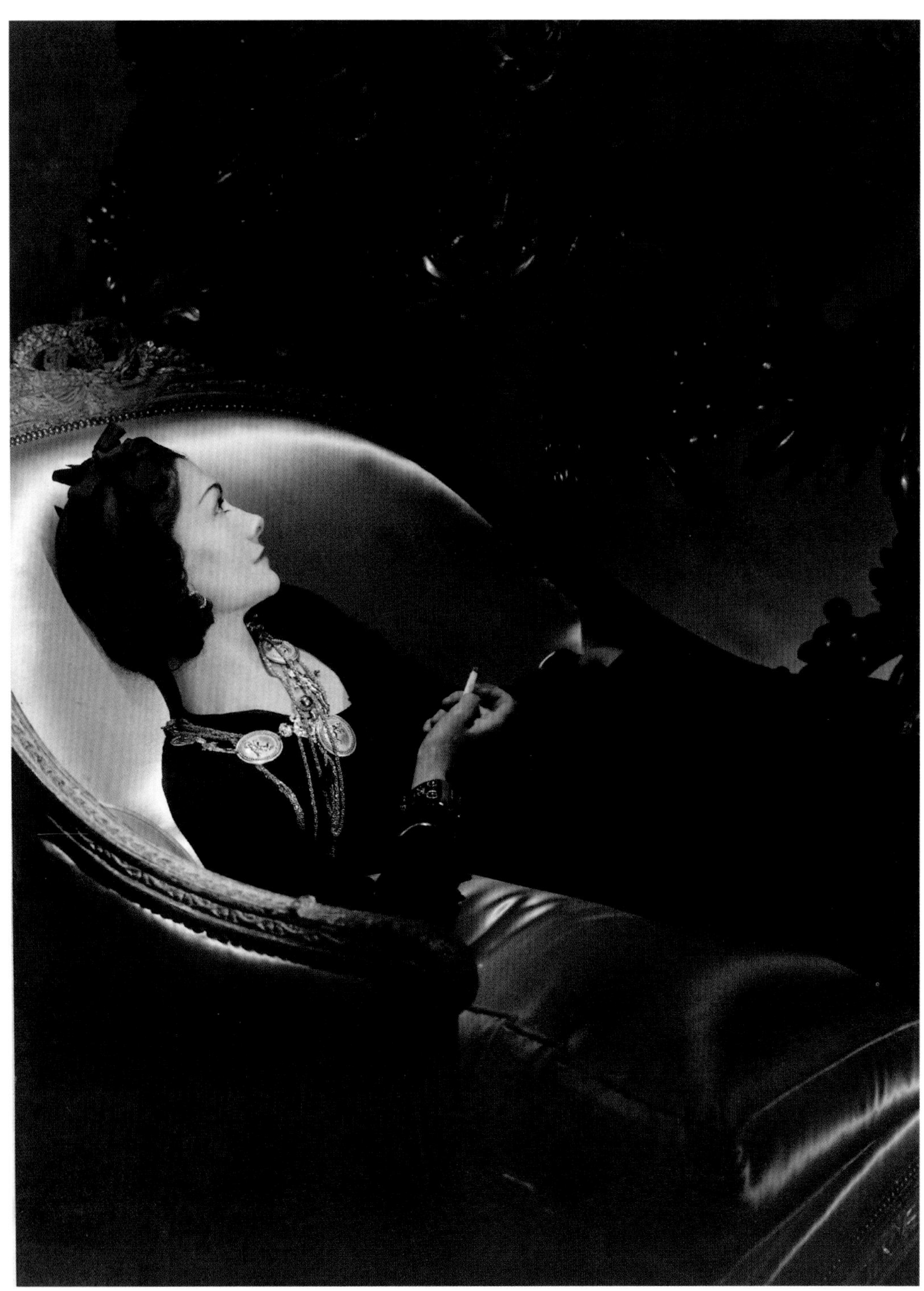

Coco Chanel, Paris, 1937

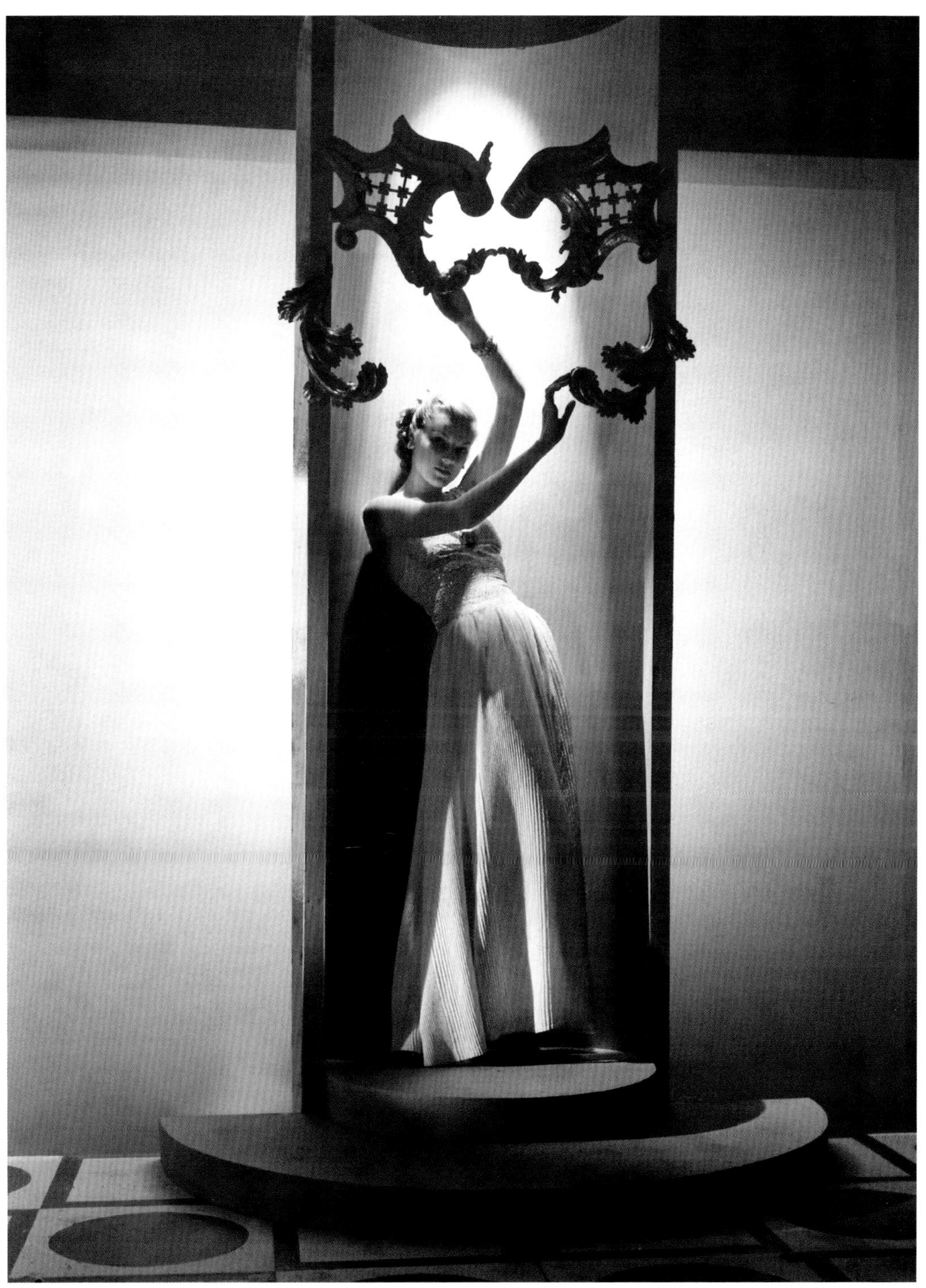

Constant, dress by Chanel, jewellery by Boucheron, 1937

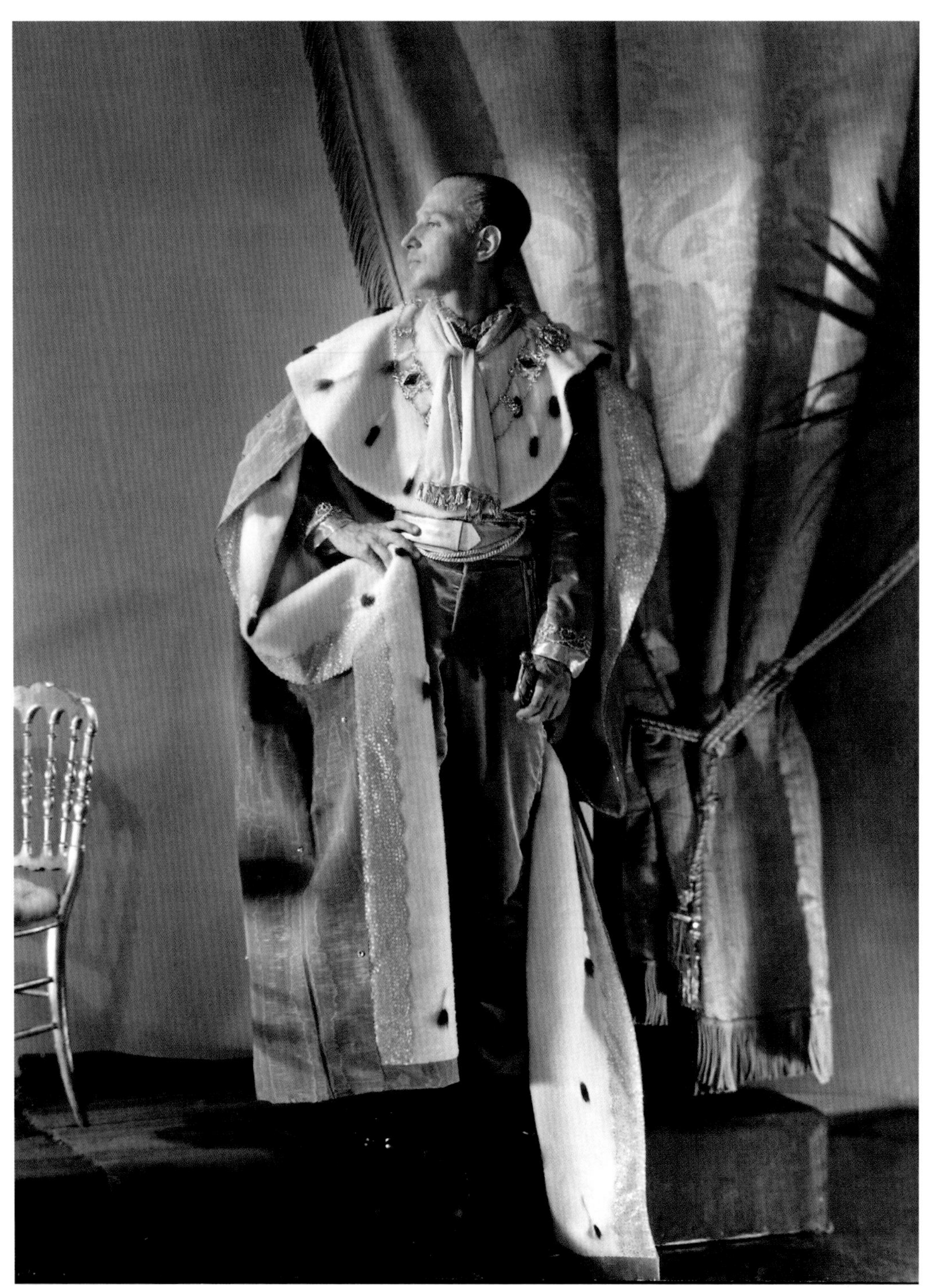

Count Charles de Beistegui, 'Bal de Valses', Paris, 1934

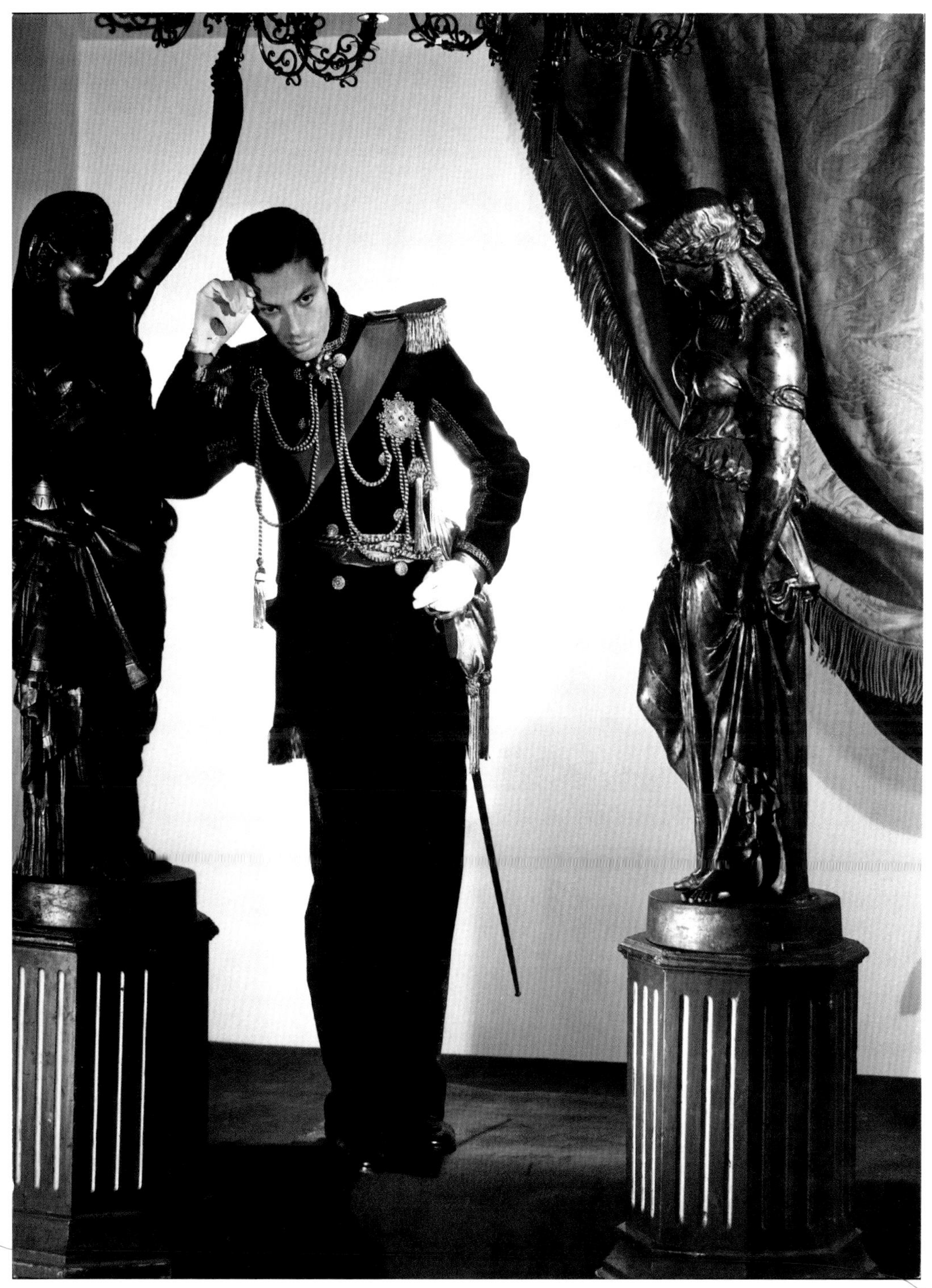

Baron Nicolas de Gunzburg, 'Bal de Valses', Paris, 1934

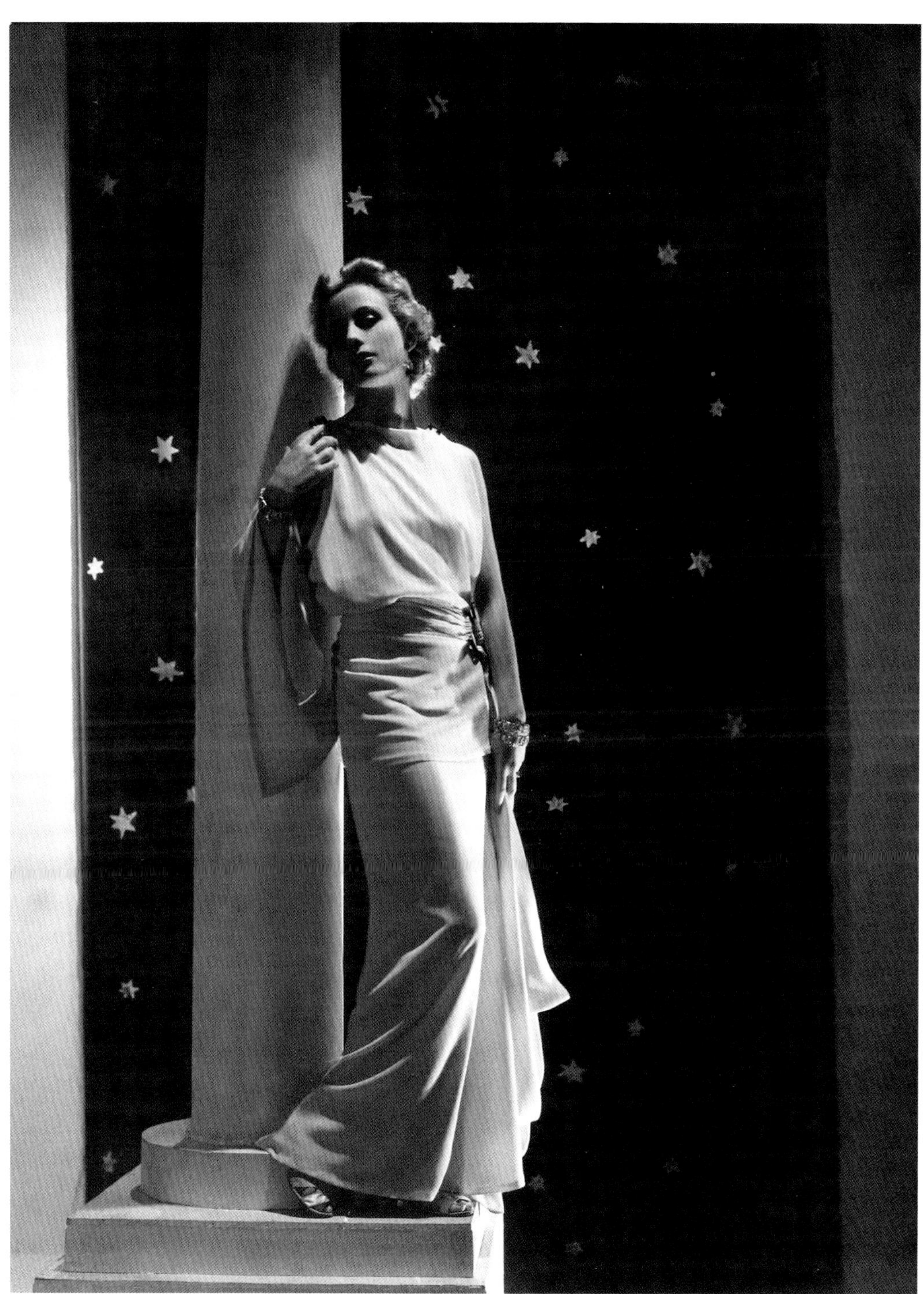

Cora Hemmet, dress by Worth, jewellery by Mauboussin, 1935

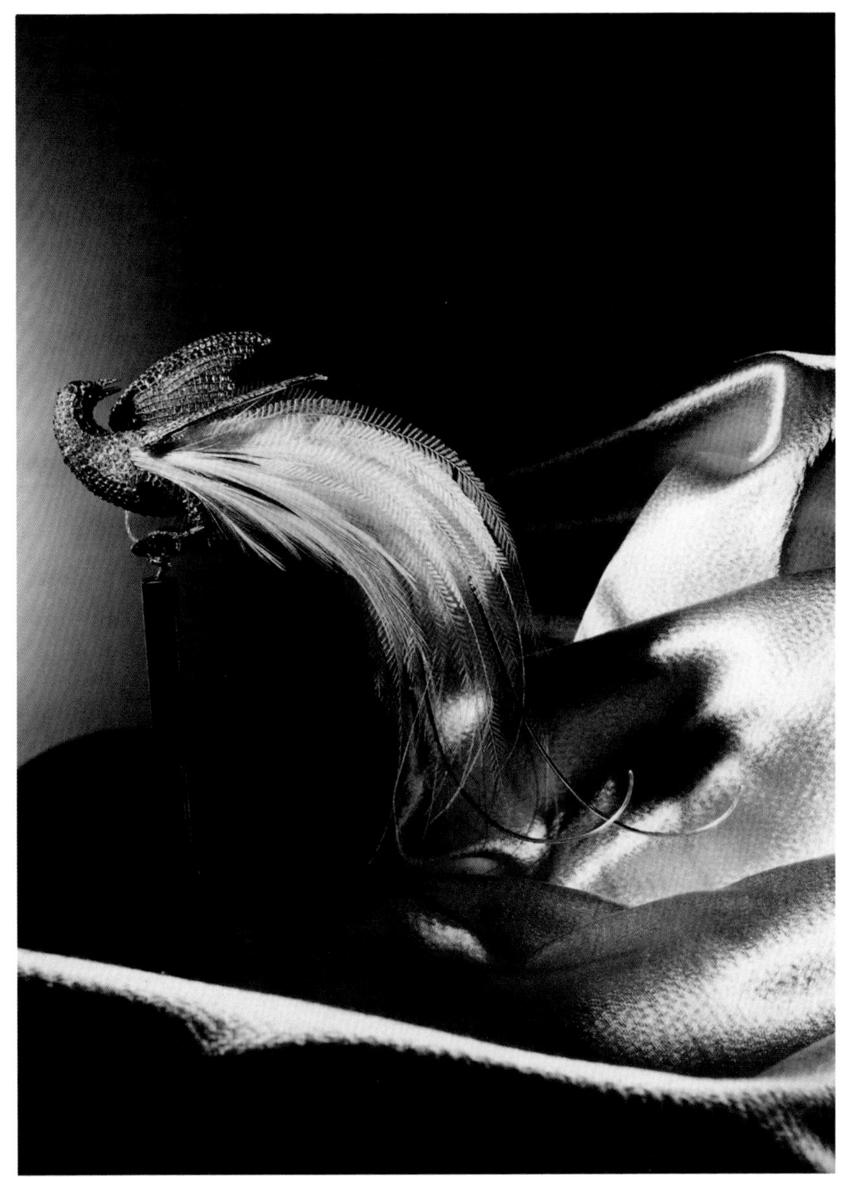

Jewellery Still Life, 1937

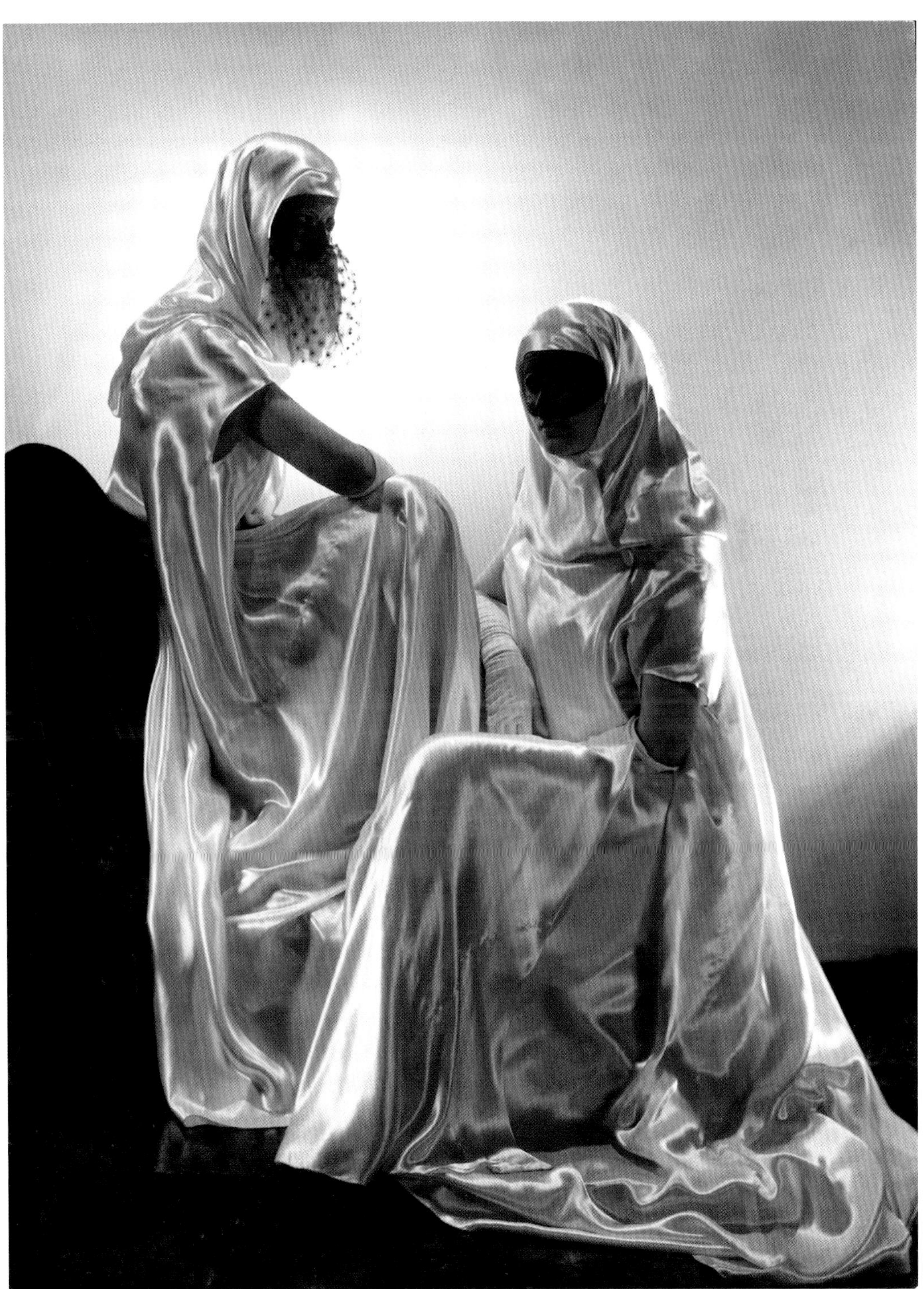

Madame Martinez de Hoz and Madame Frédéric Bemberg, 1934

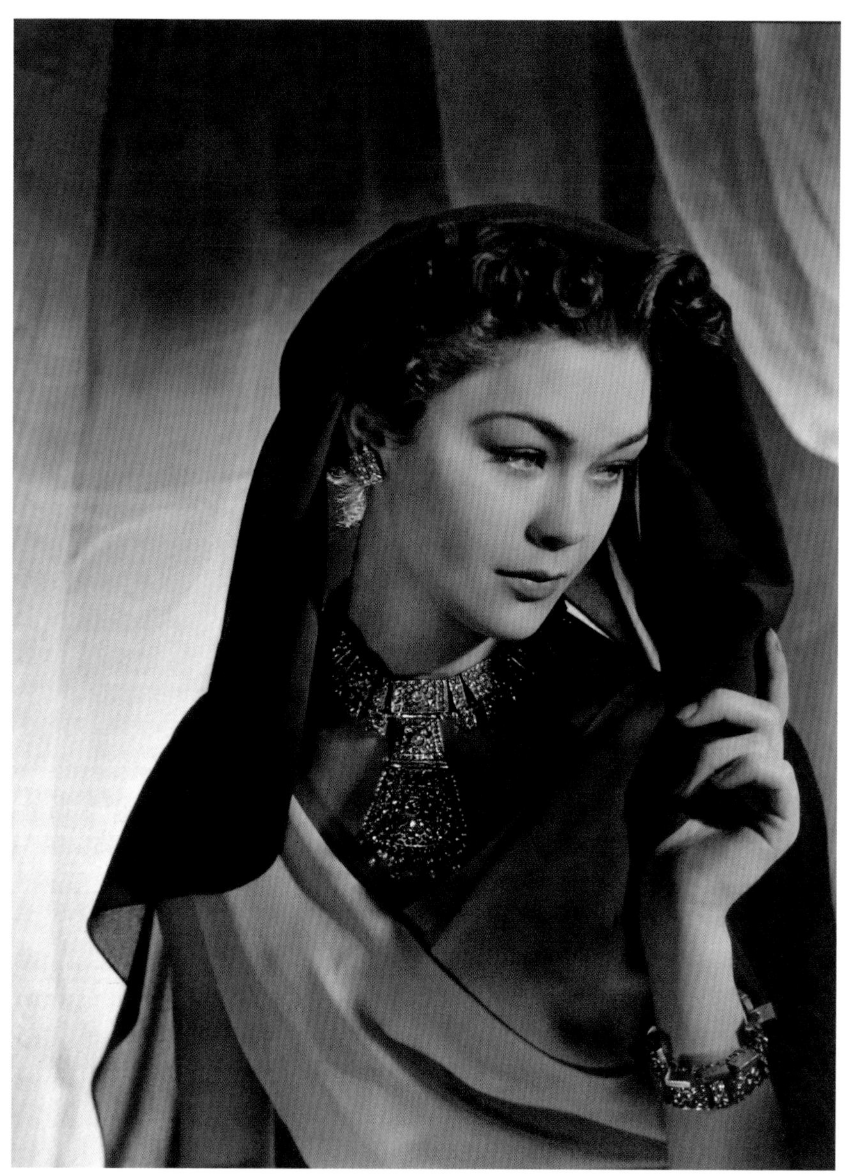

Lud, dress by Schiaparelli, jewellery by Cartier, 1935

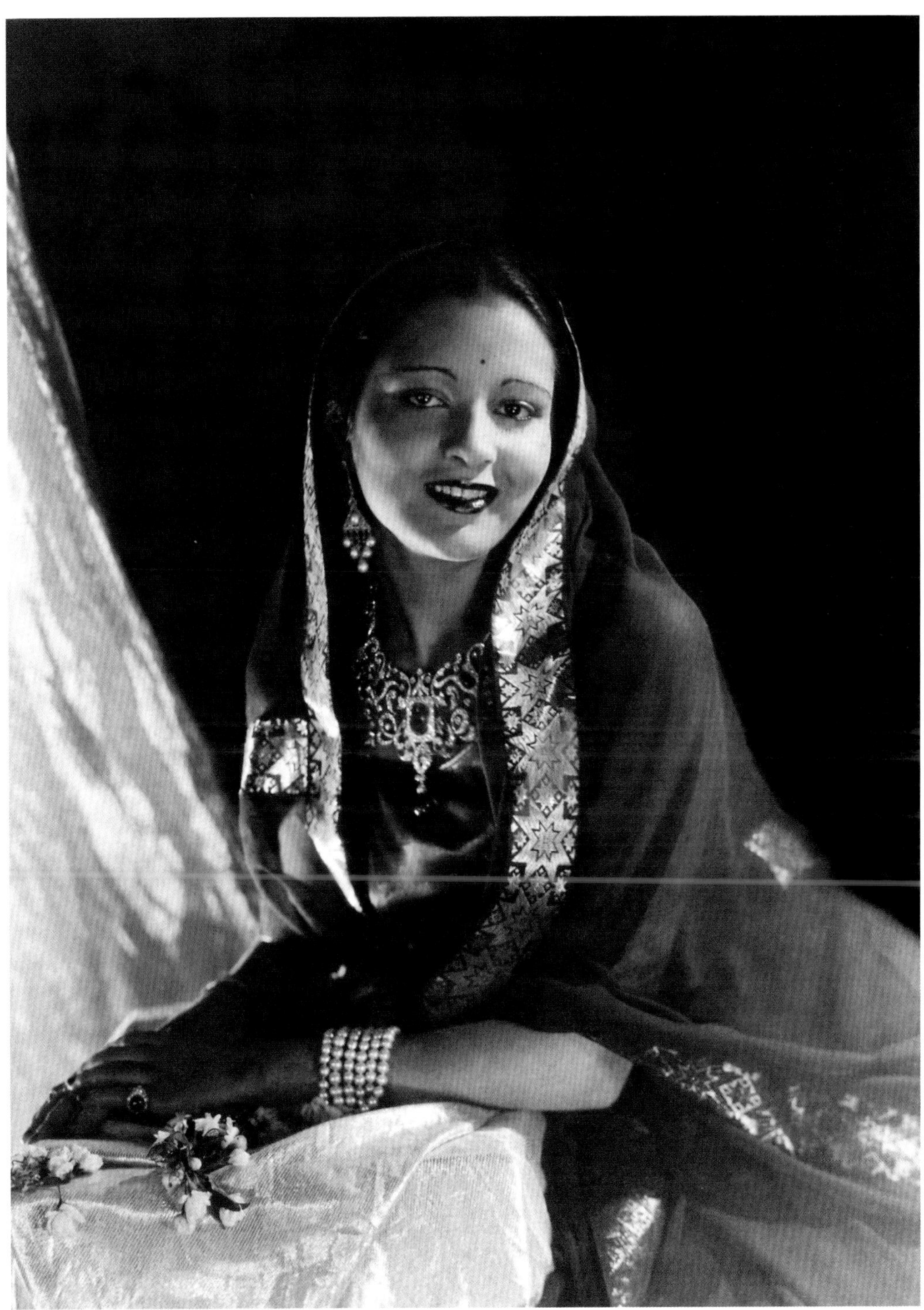

Princess Karam of Kapurthala, London, 1934

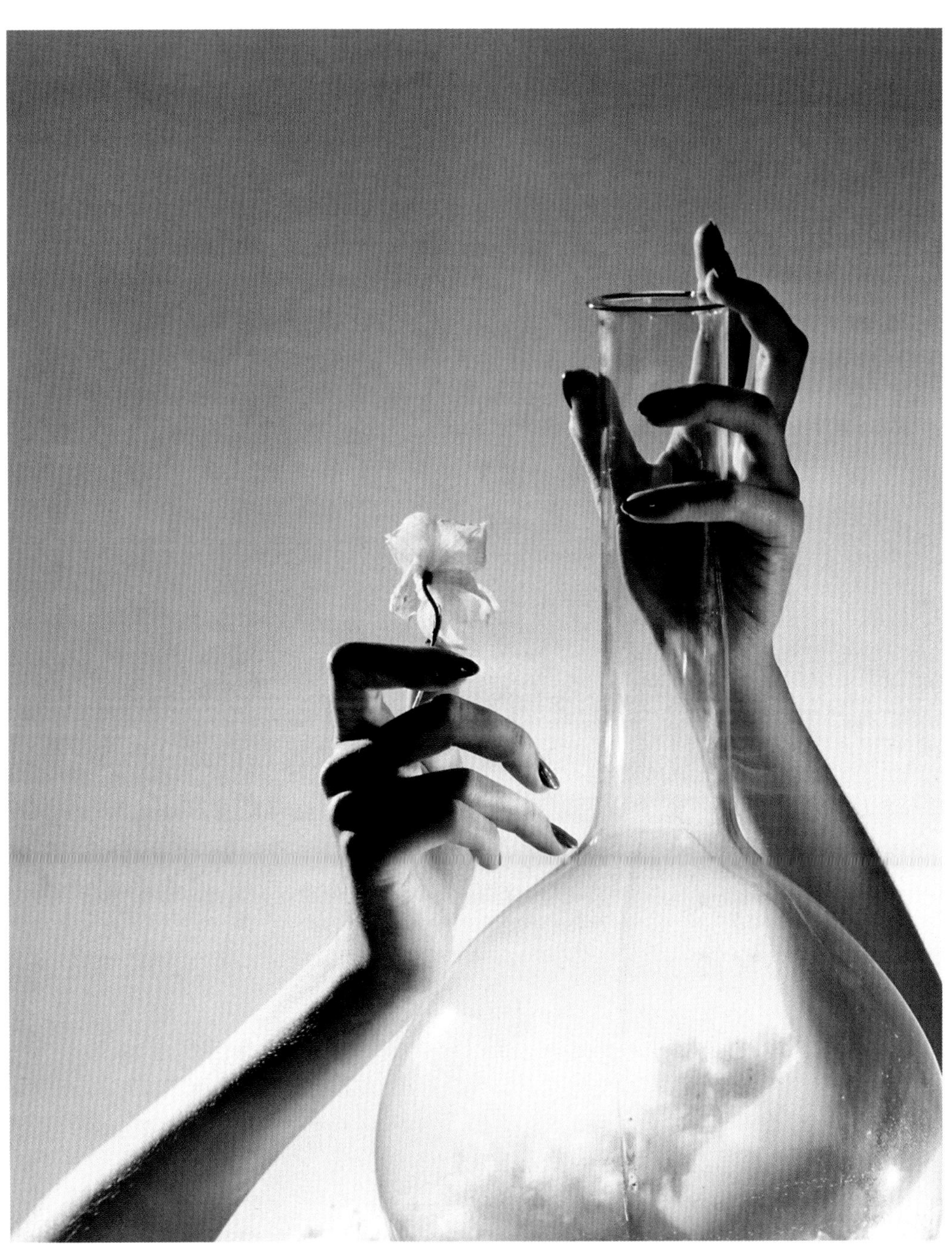

Lisa Fonssagrives, *Hands and Vase*, 1941

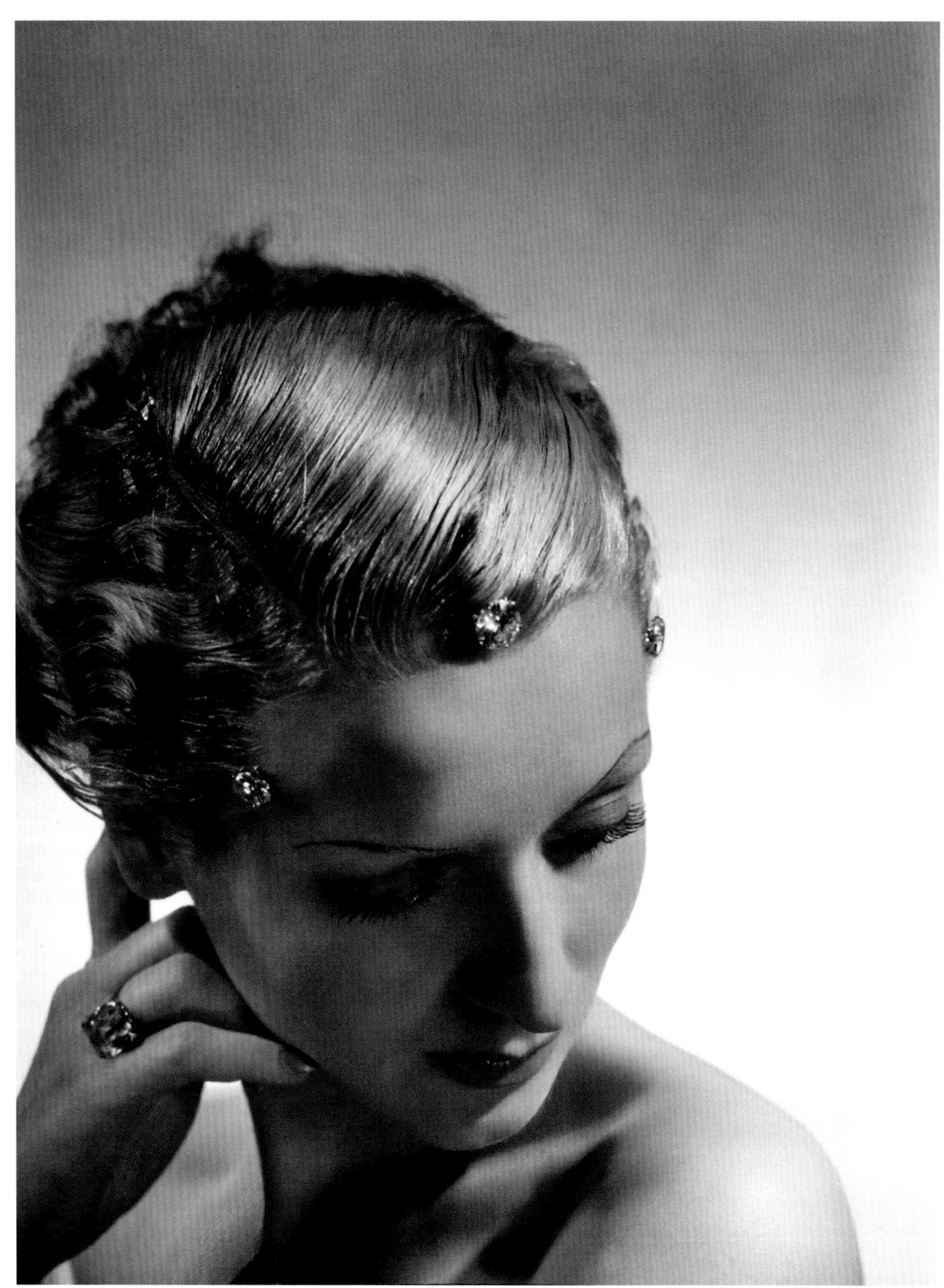

Mary Stutz, jewellery by Cartier, 1934

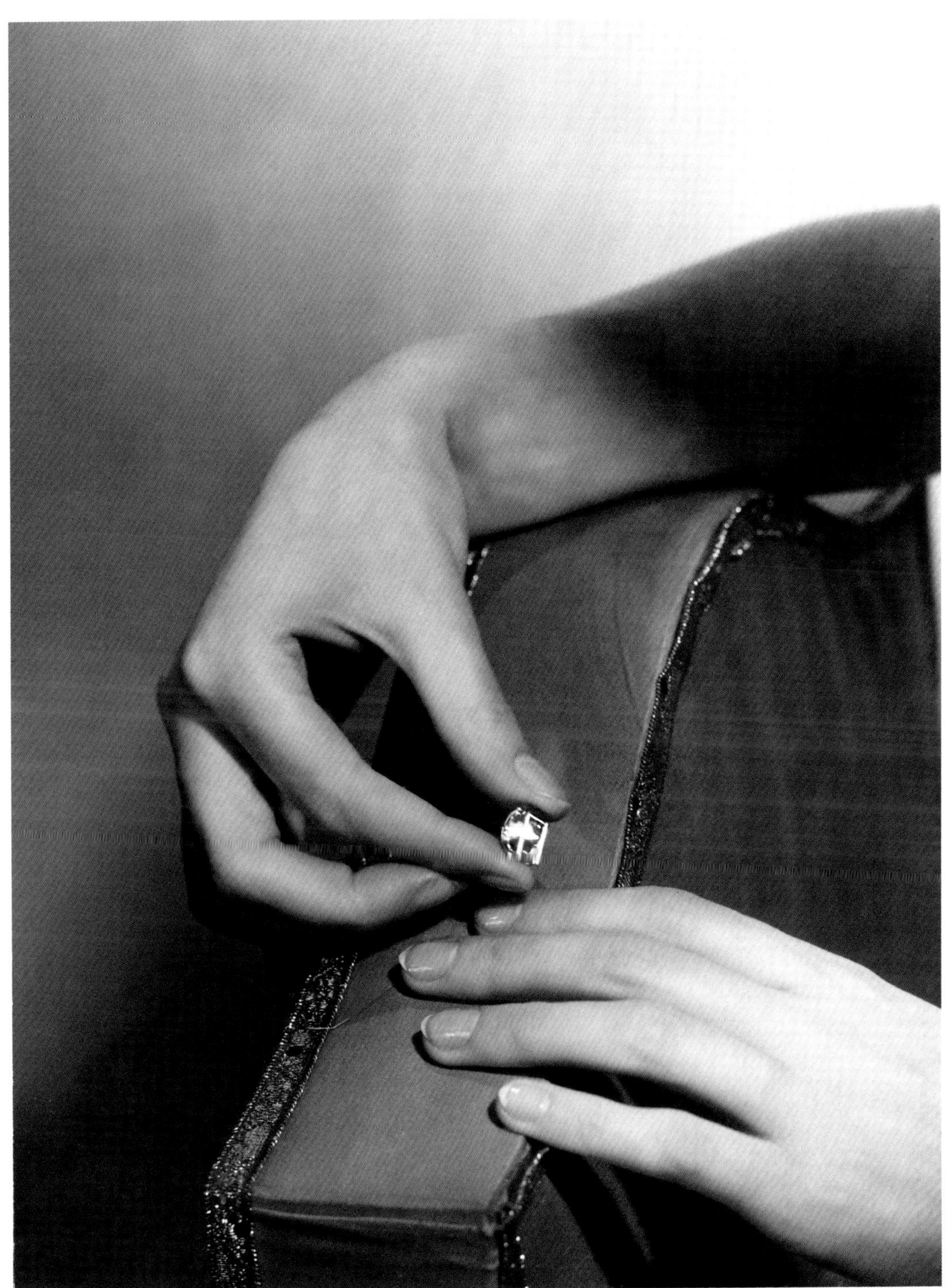

Mary Stutz, jewellery by Cartier, 1934

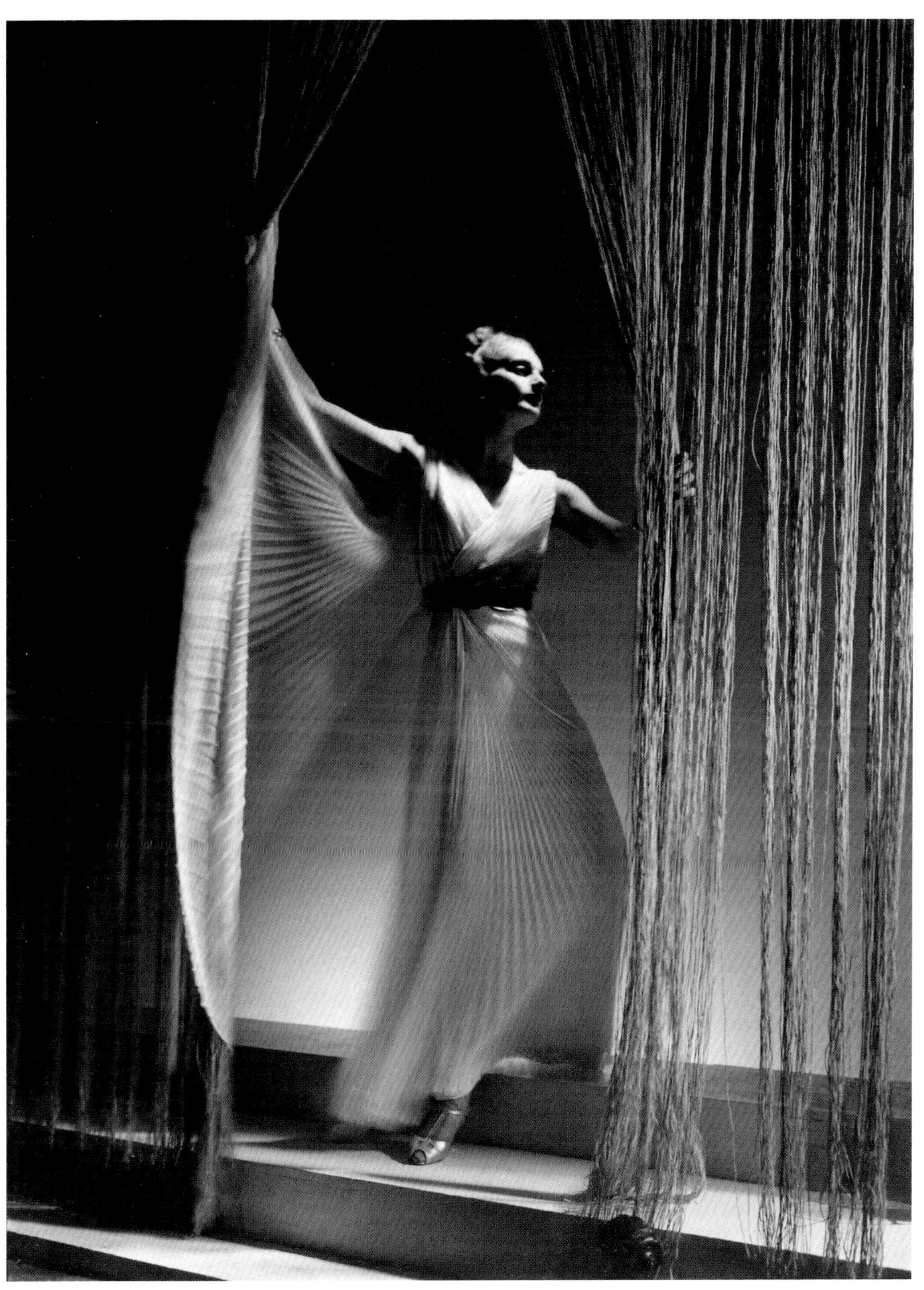

Lyla Zelensky, dress by Jean Patou, jewellery by Mauboussin, 1937

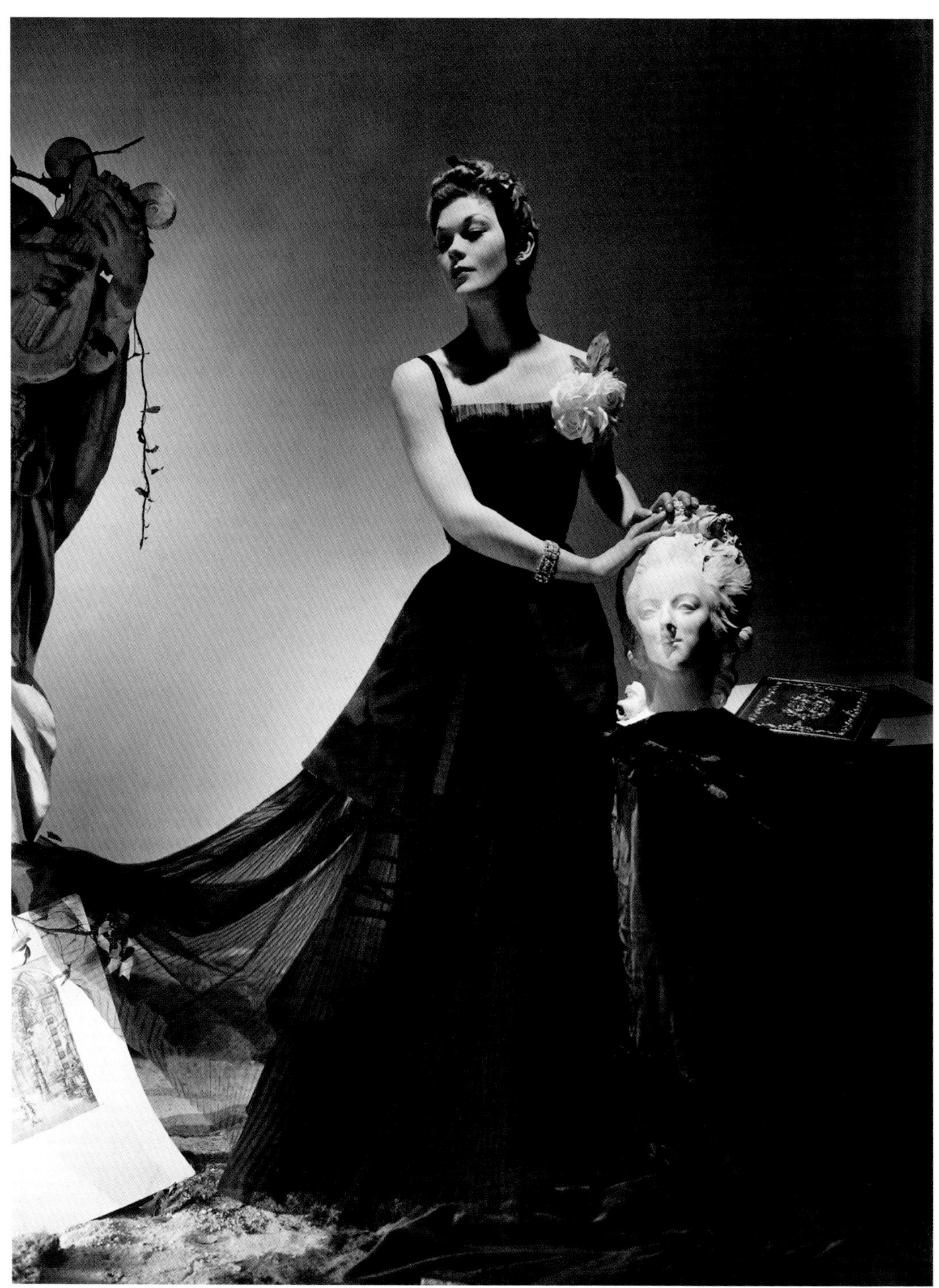

Lud, dress by Jean Patou, jewellery by Mauboussin, 1938

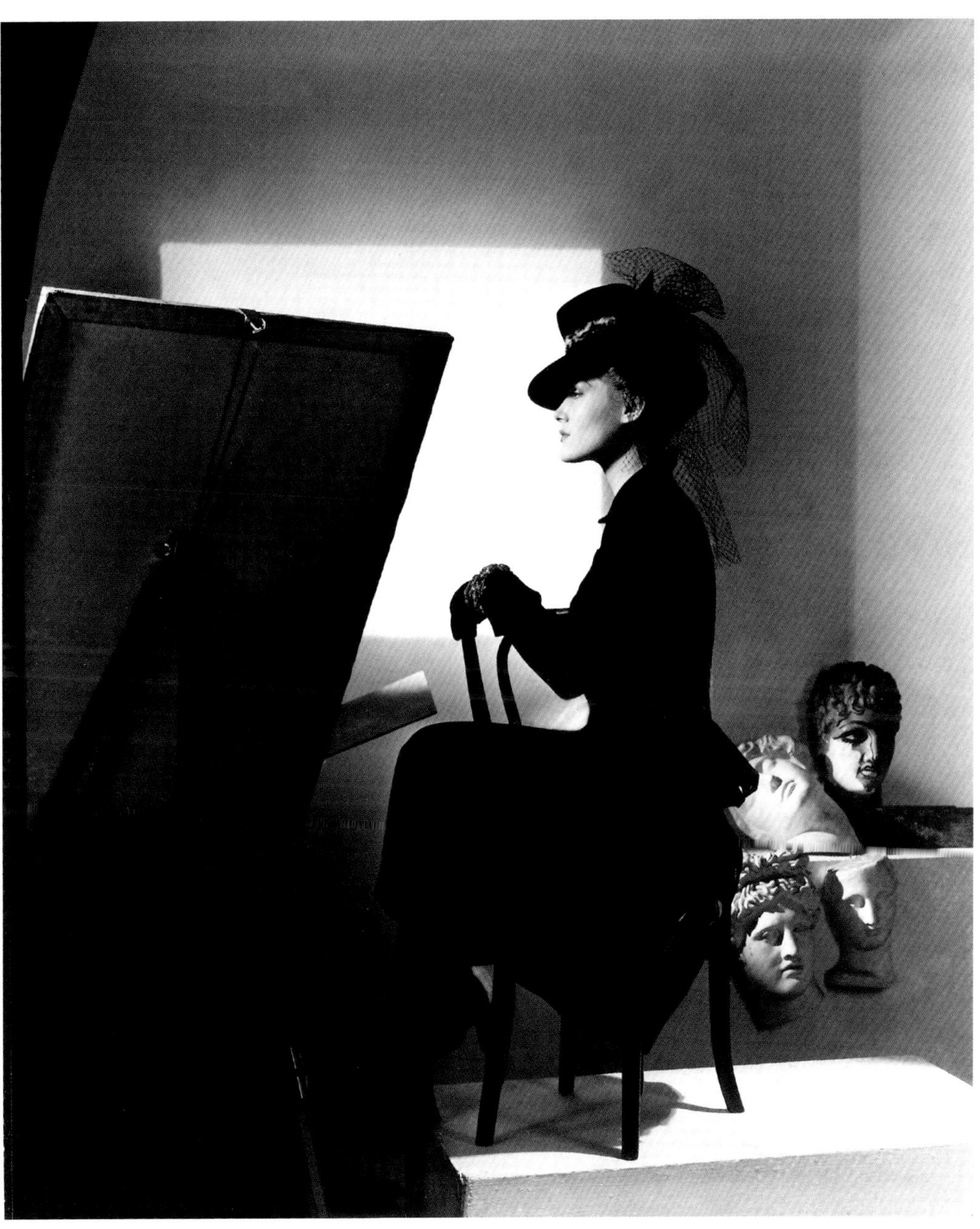

Estrella Boissevain, hat and coat-dress by Bergdorf Goodman, 1938

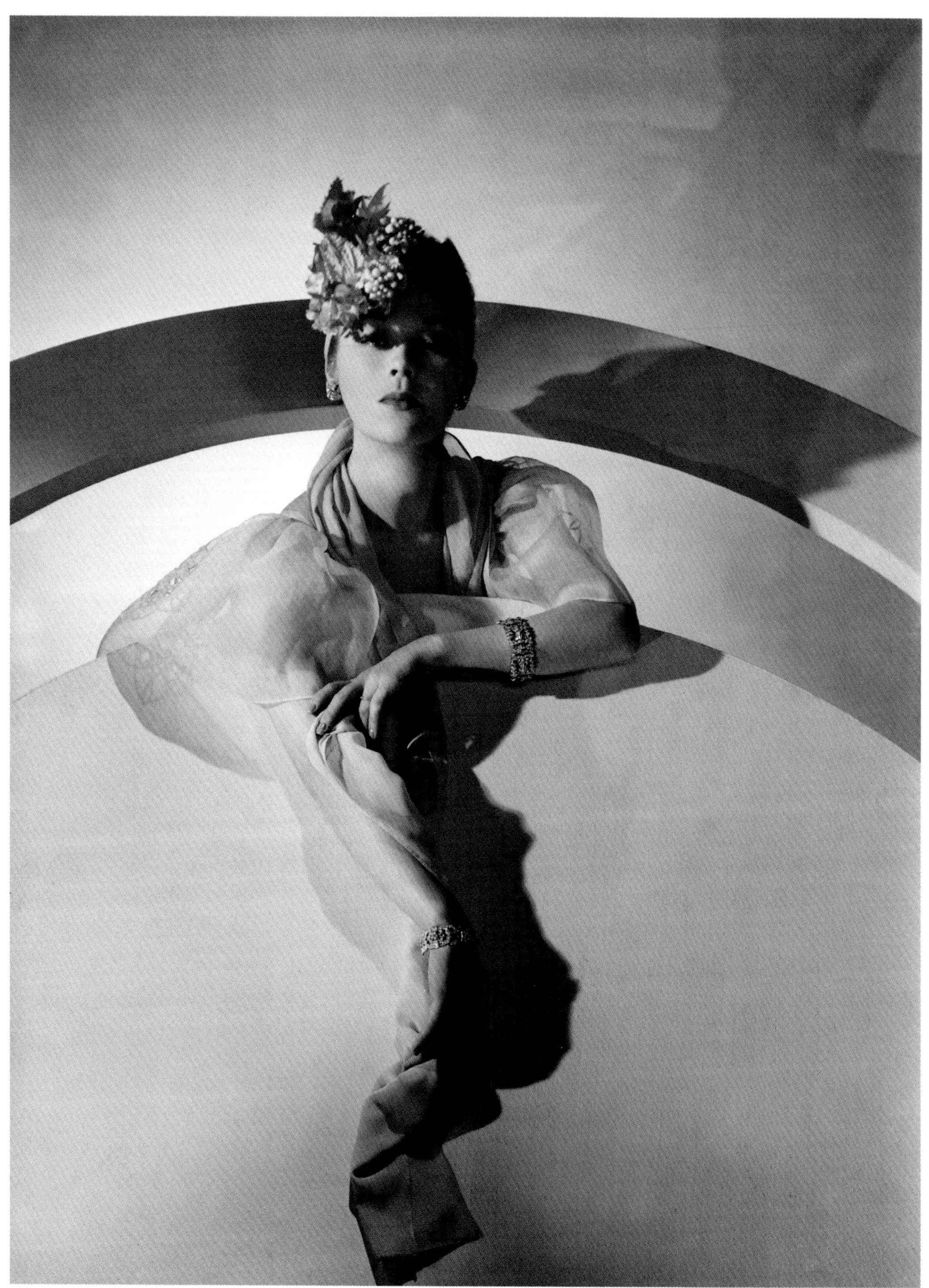

Lud, corsage by Lanvin, jewellery by Mauboussin, 1938

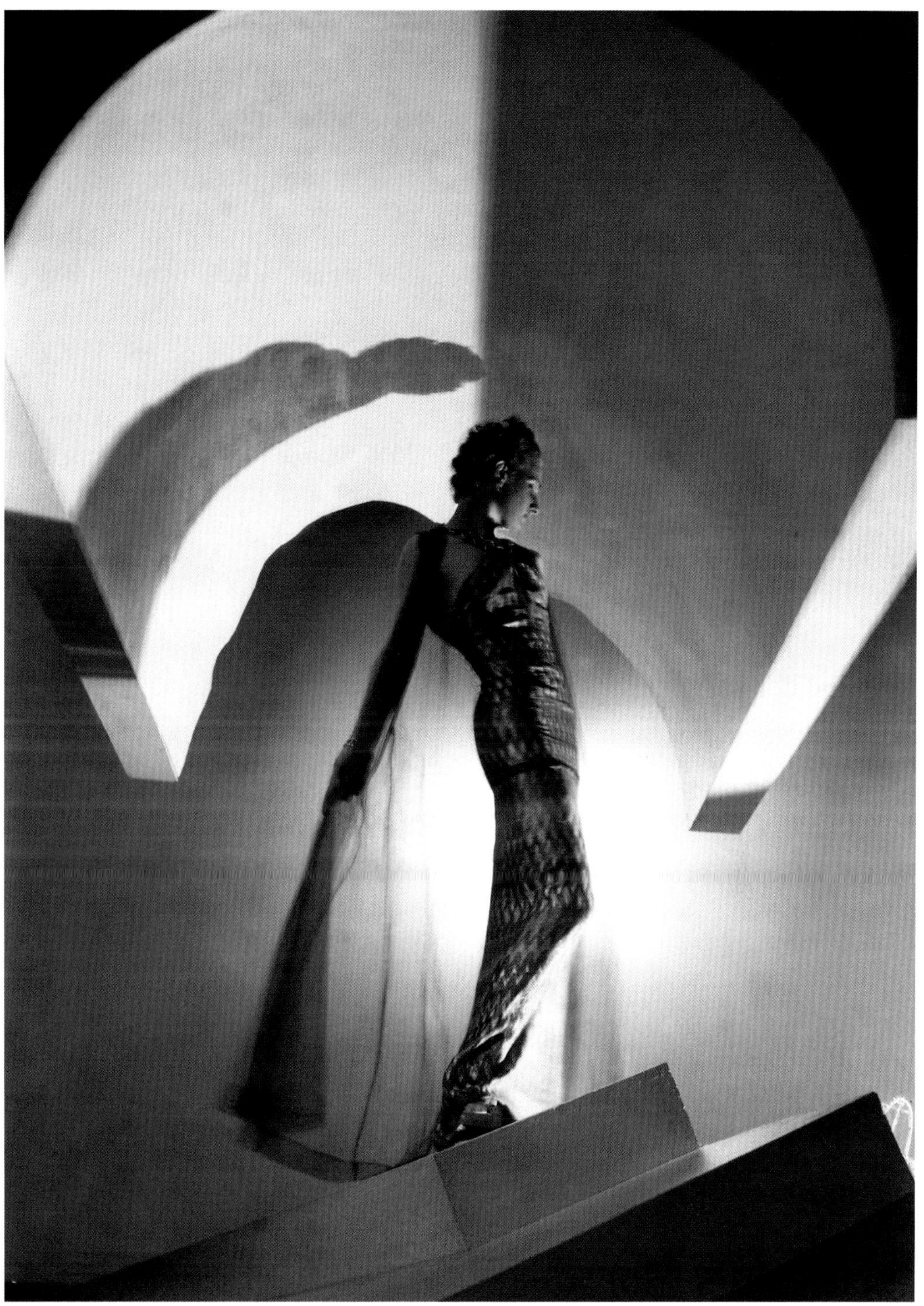

Lyla Zelensky, dress by Molyneux, jewellery by Boucheron, 1937

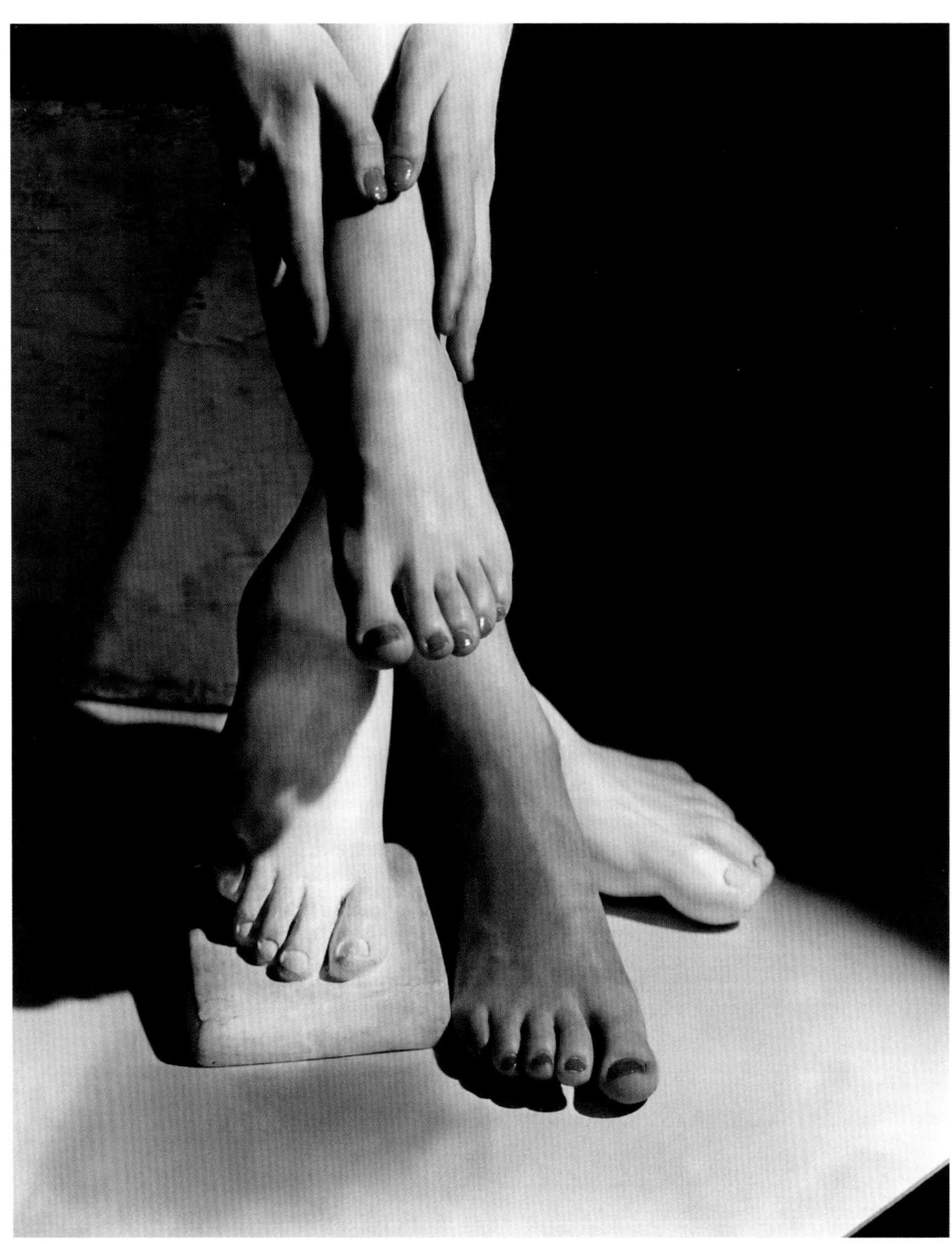

Barefoot Beauty, 1941

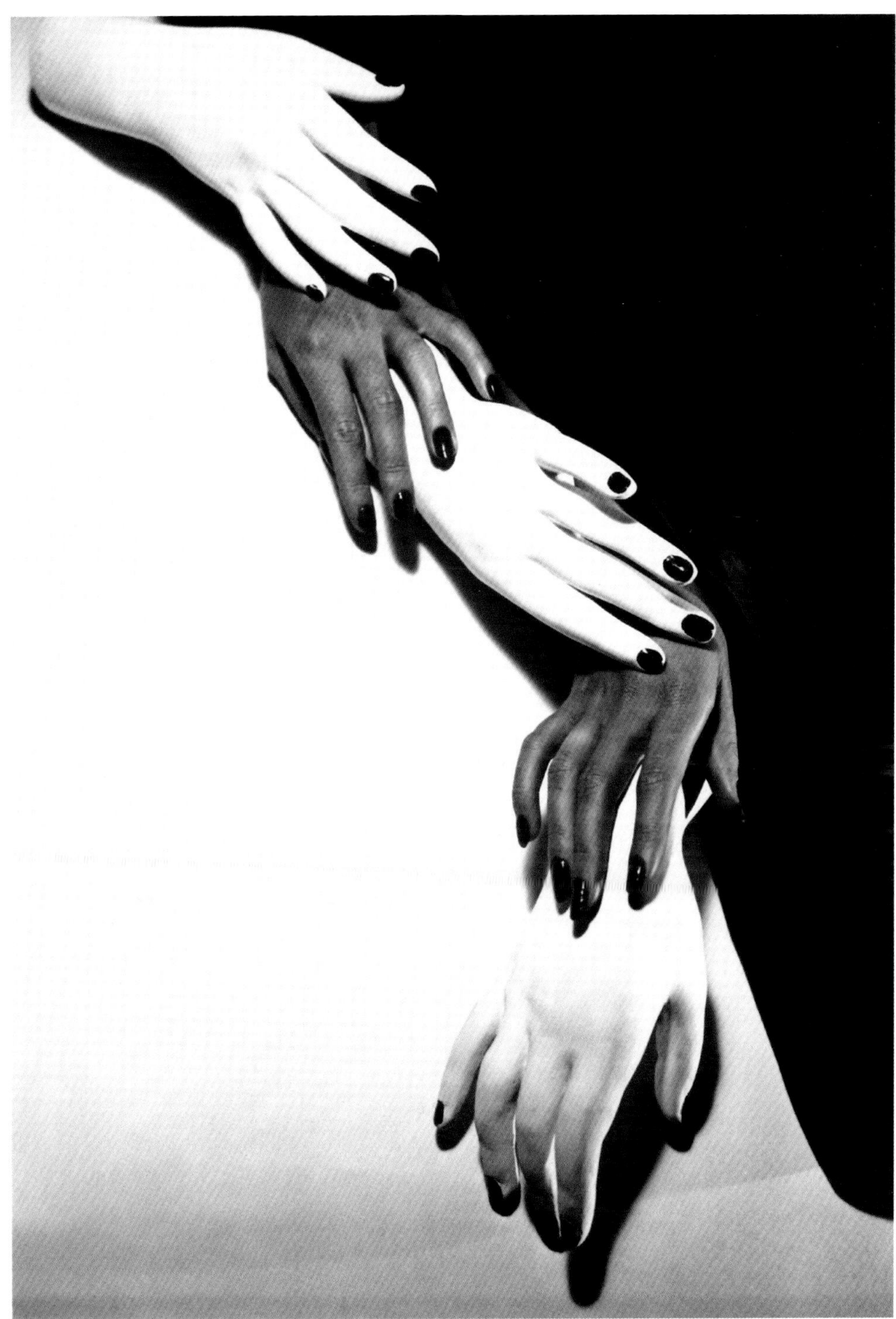

Hands, Hands, Hands, 1941

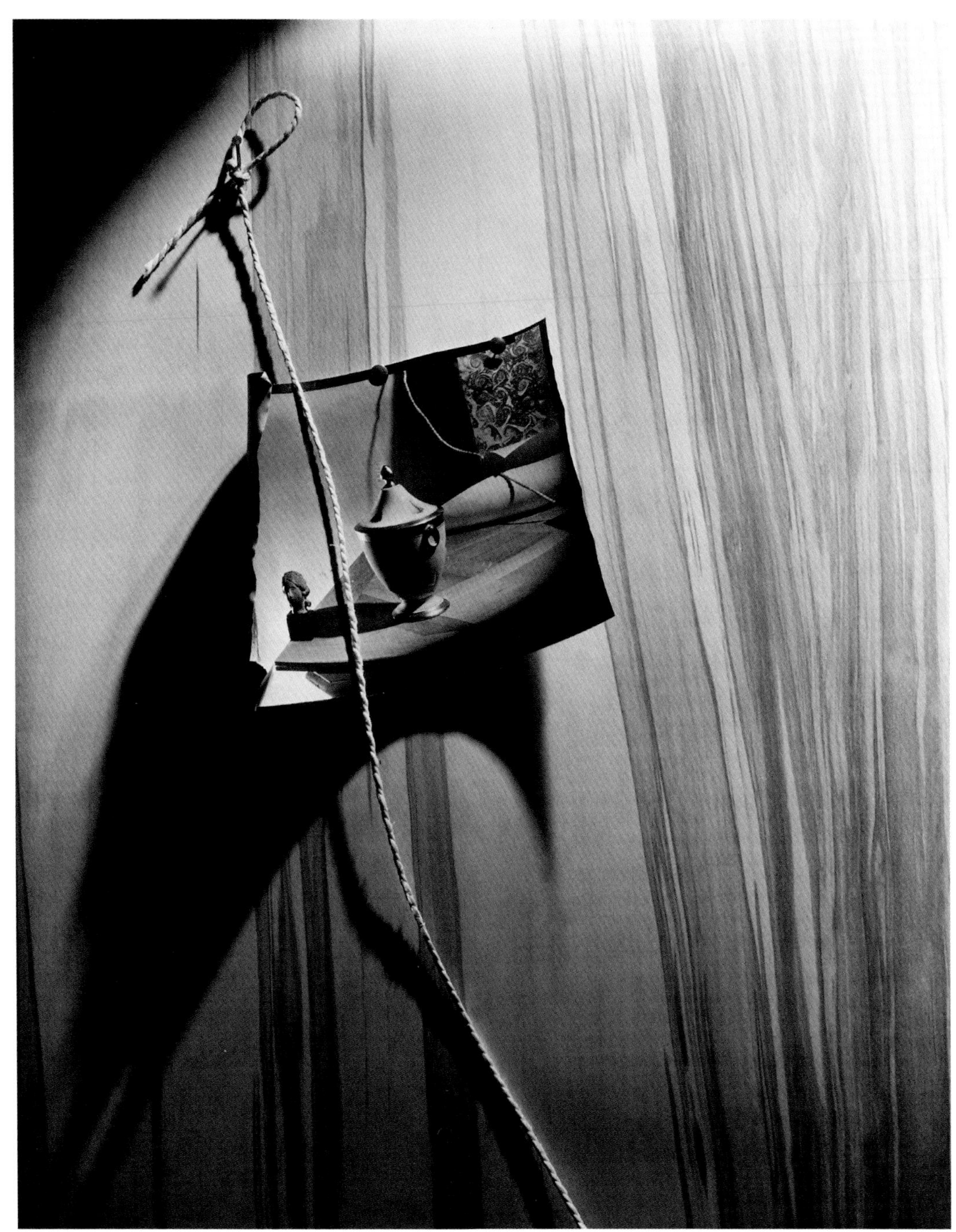

Still Life, 1942

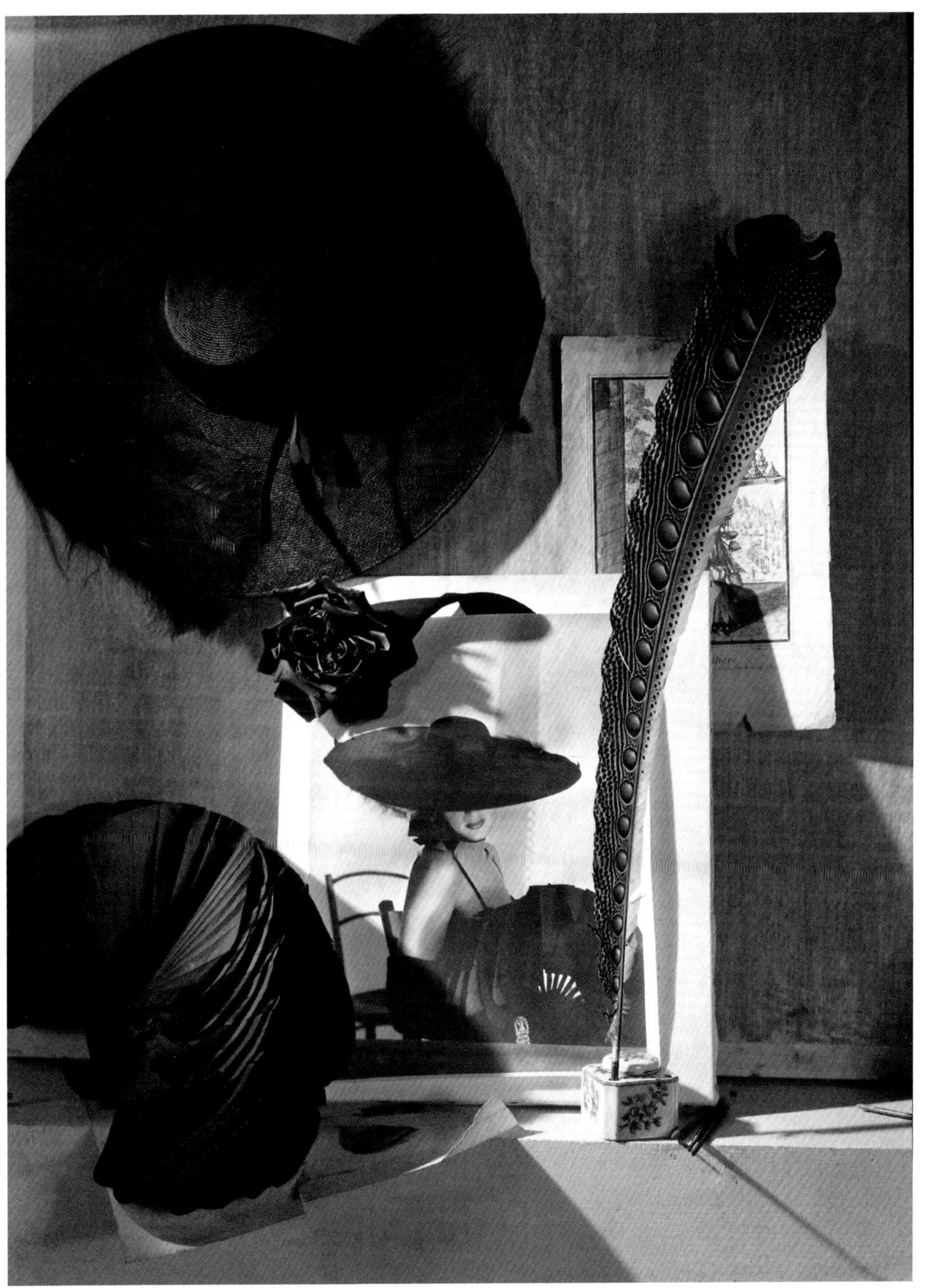

Marquise de Montesquiou-Fezensac, accessories by Molyneux, 1938

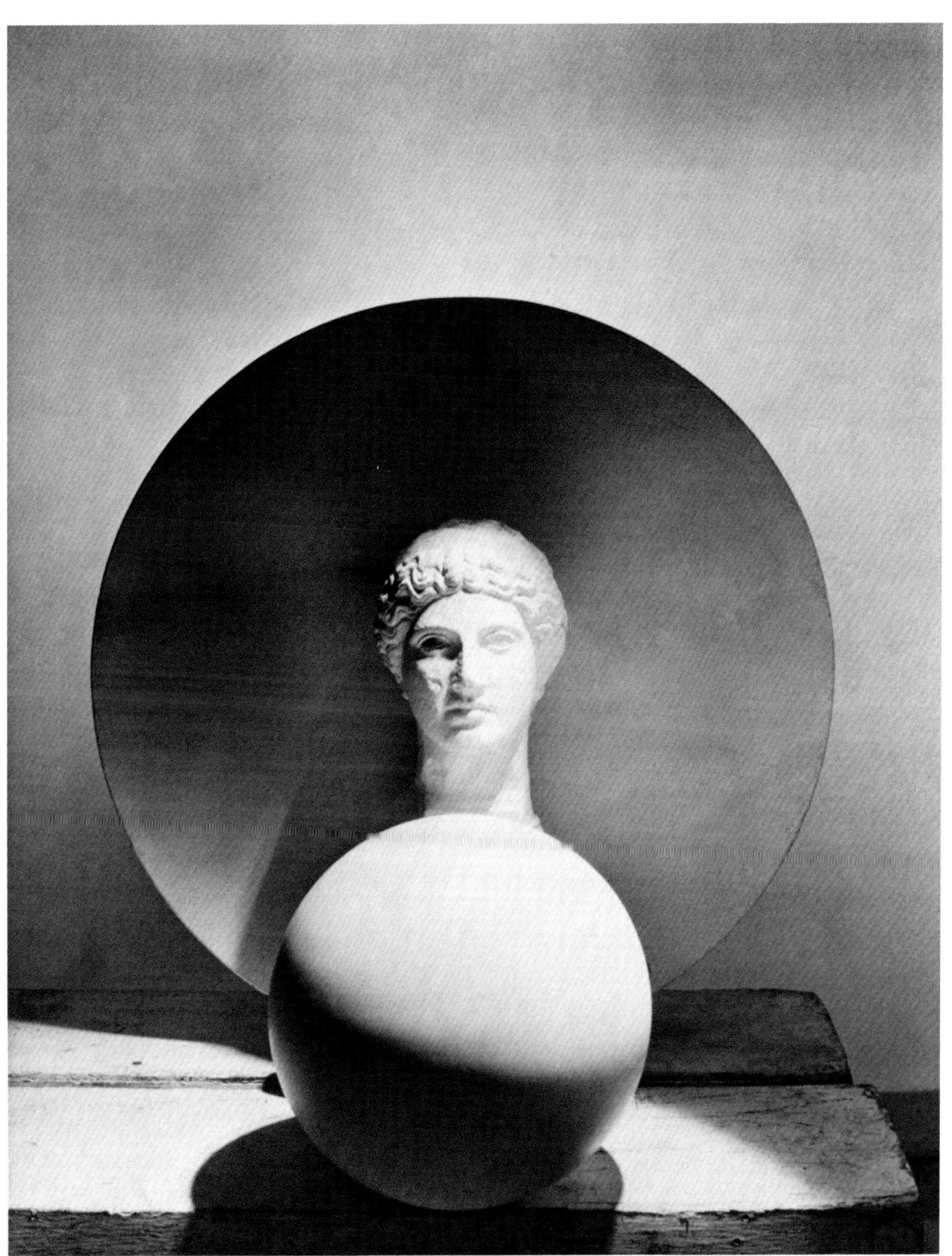
Classical Still Life, 1937

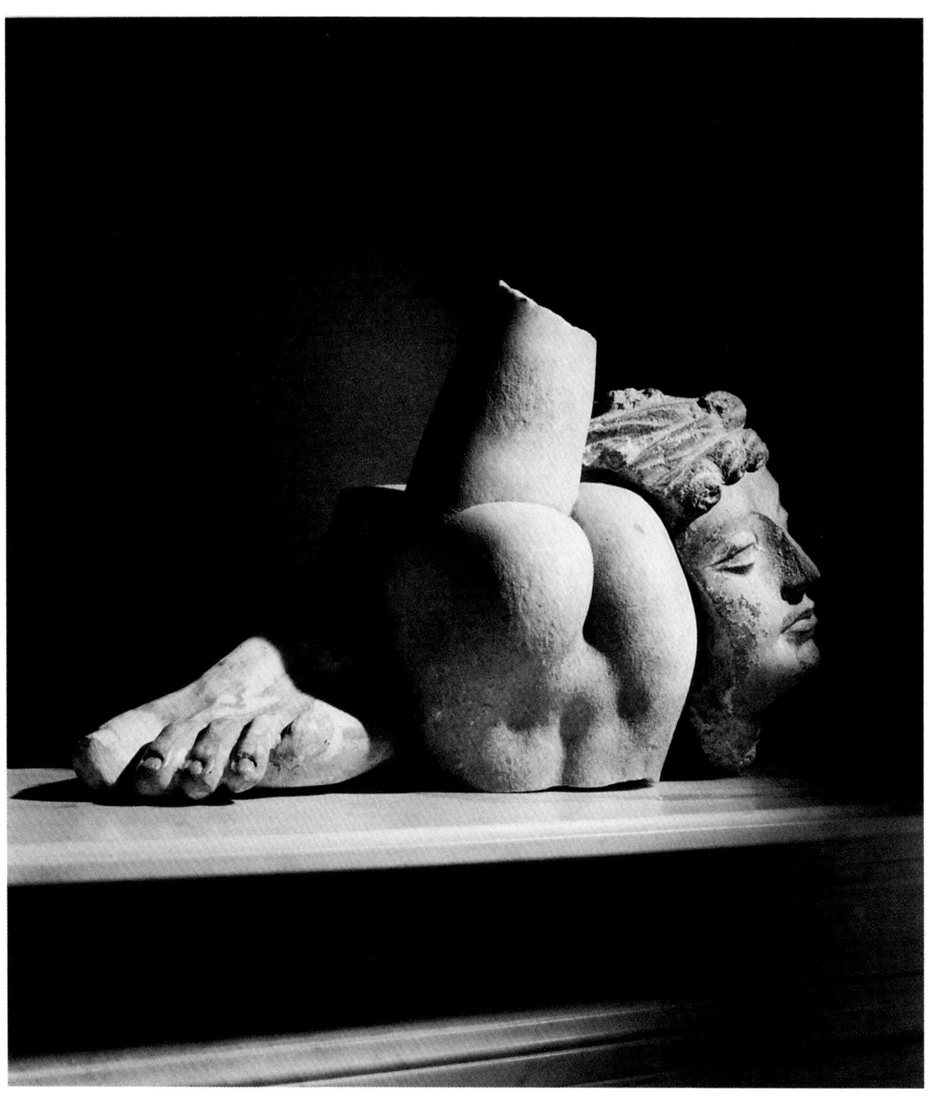

Body Parts, Still Life, 1989

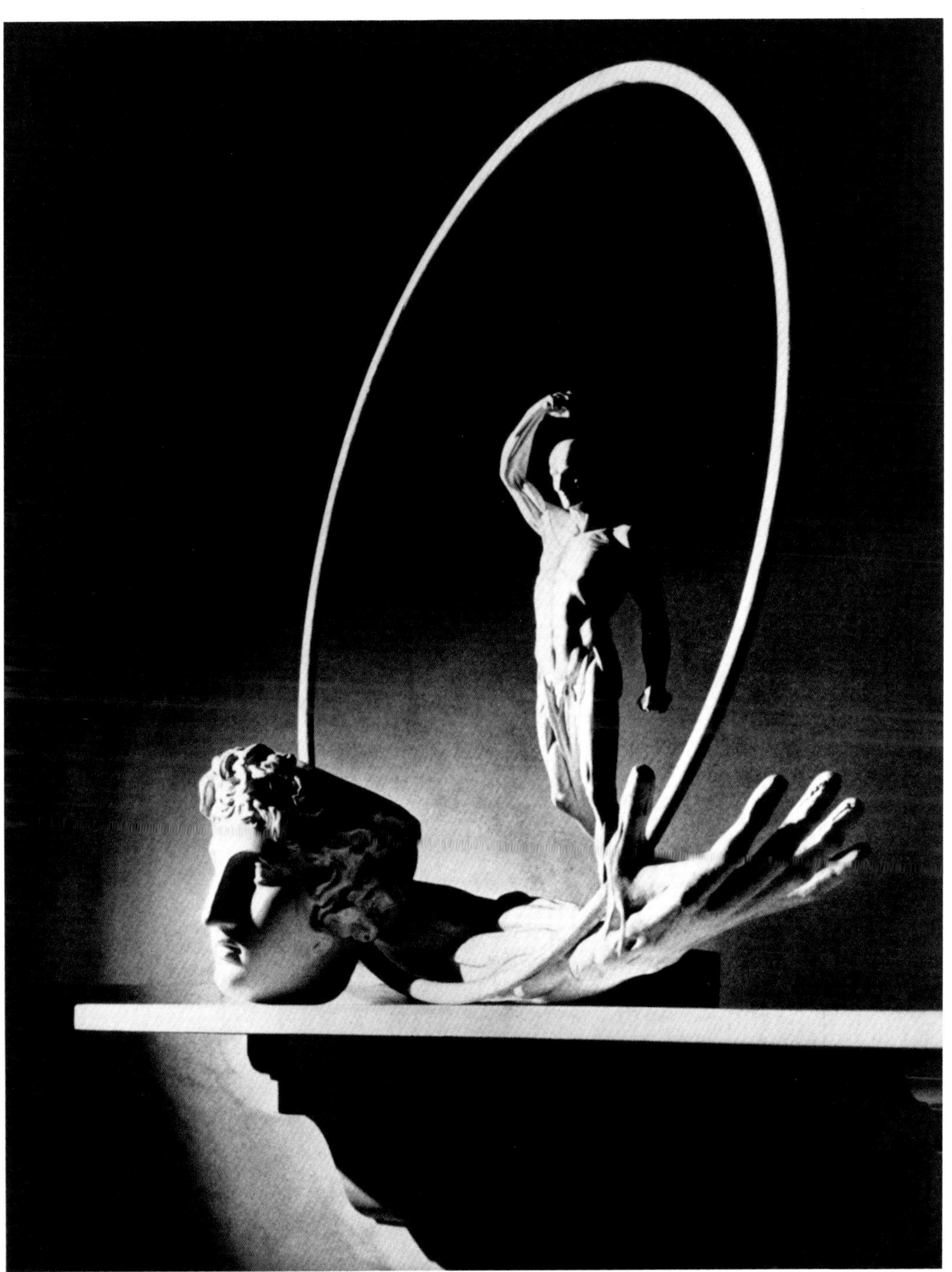

Houdon Still Life, 1939

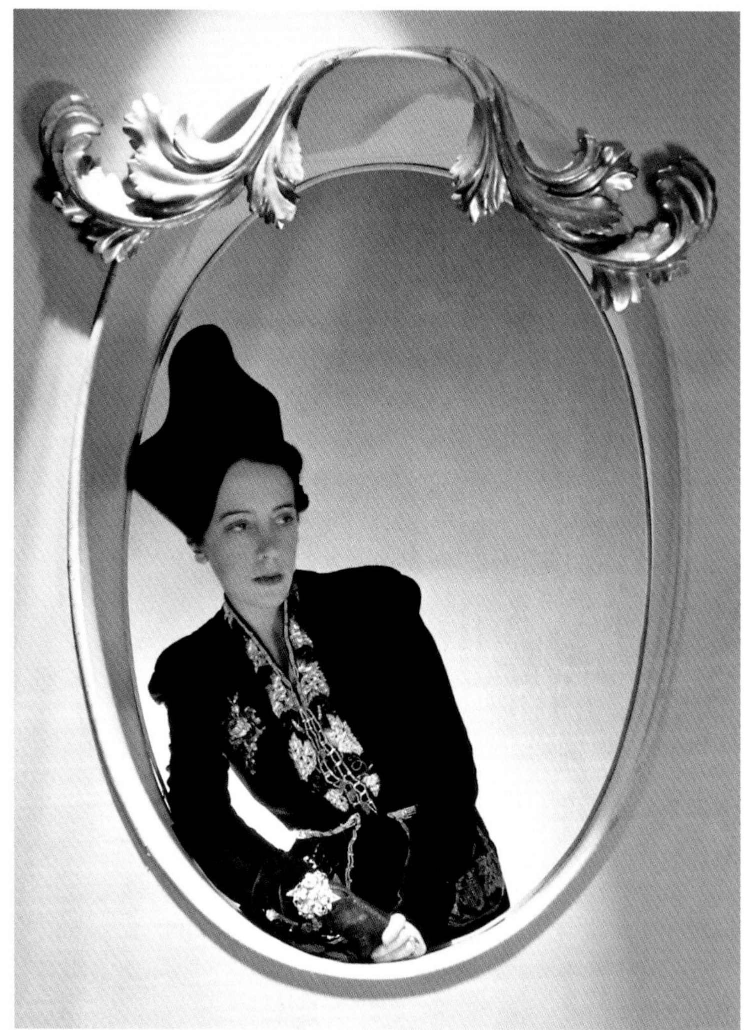

Elsa Schiaparelli, Paris, 1937

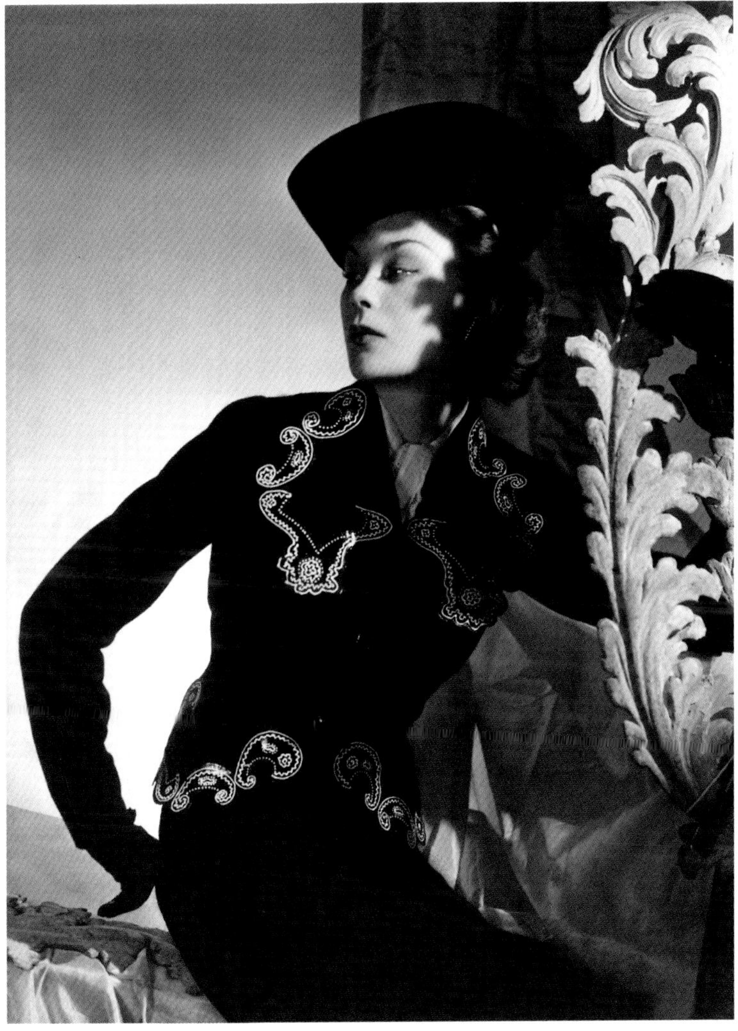

Lud, suit and hat by Schiaparelli, jewellery by Mauboussin, 1937

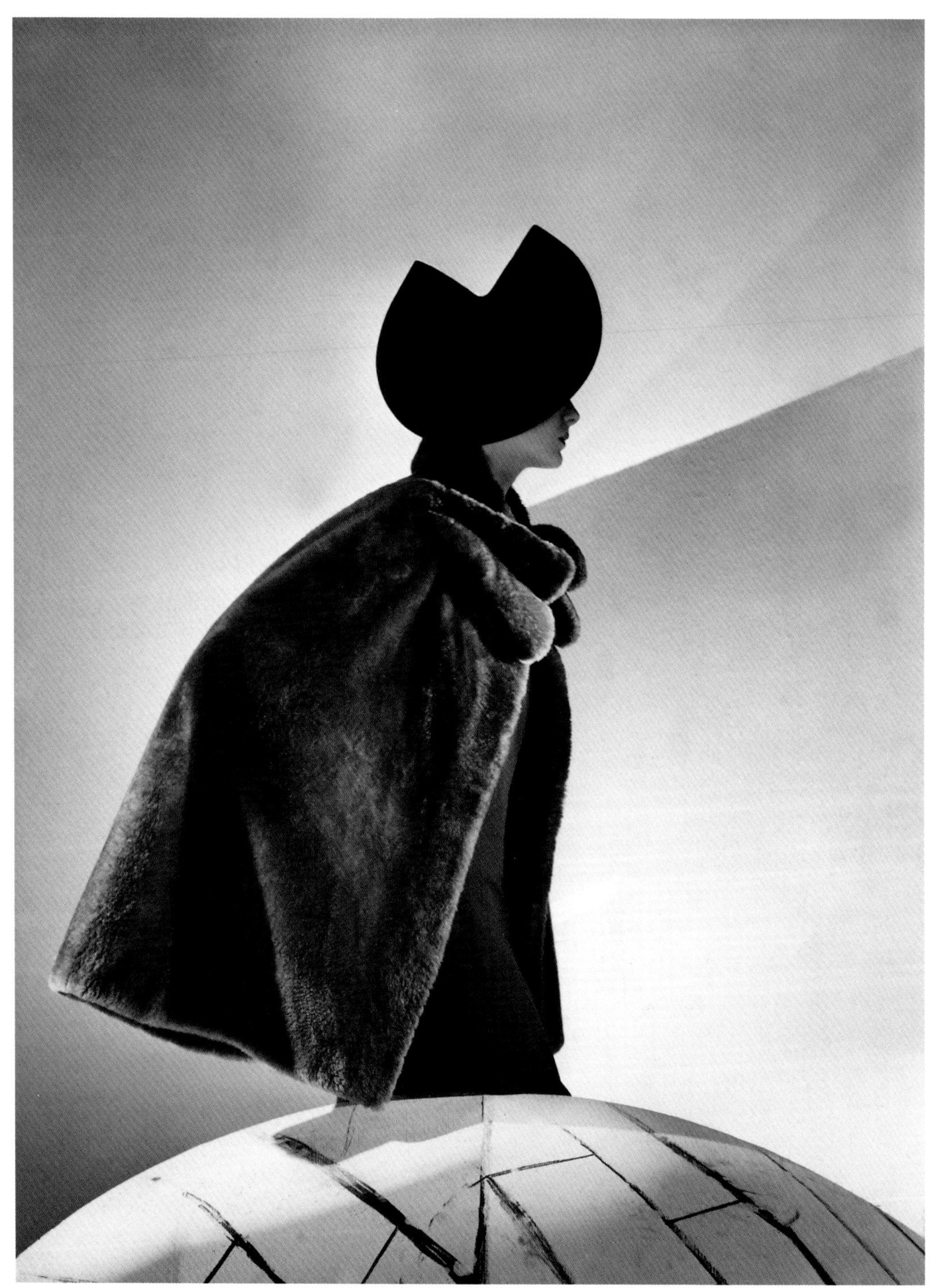

Mary Belevsky, beret and cape by Lanvin, jewellery by Boucheron, 1938

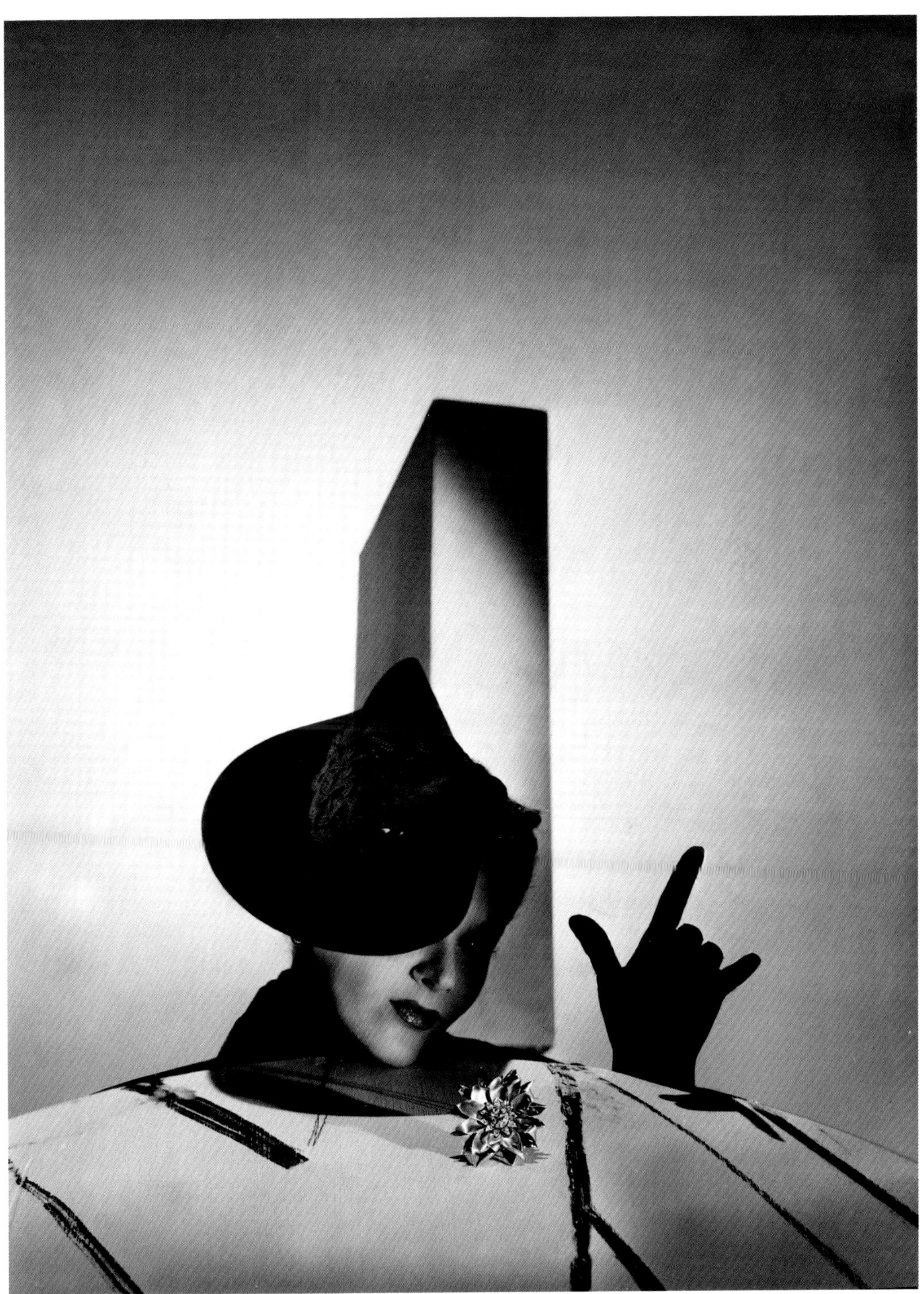

Lisa Fonssagrives, hat by Suzy, jewellery by Boucheron, 1938

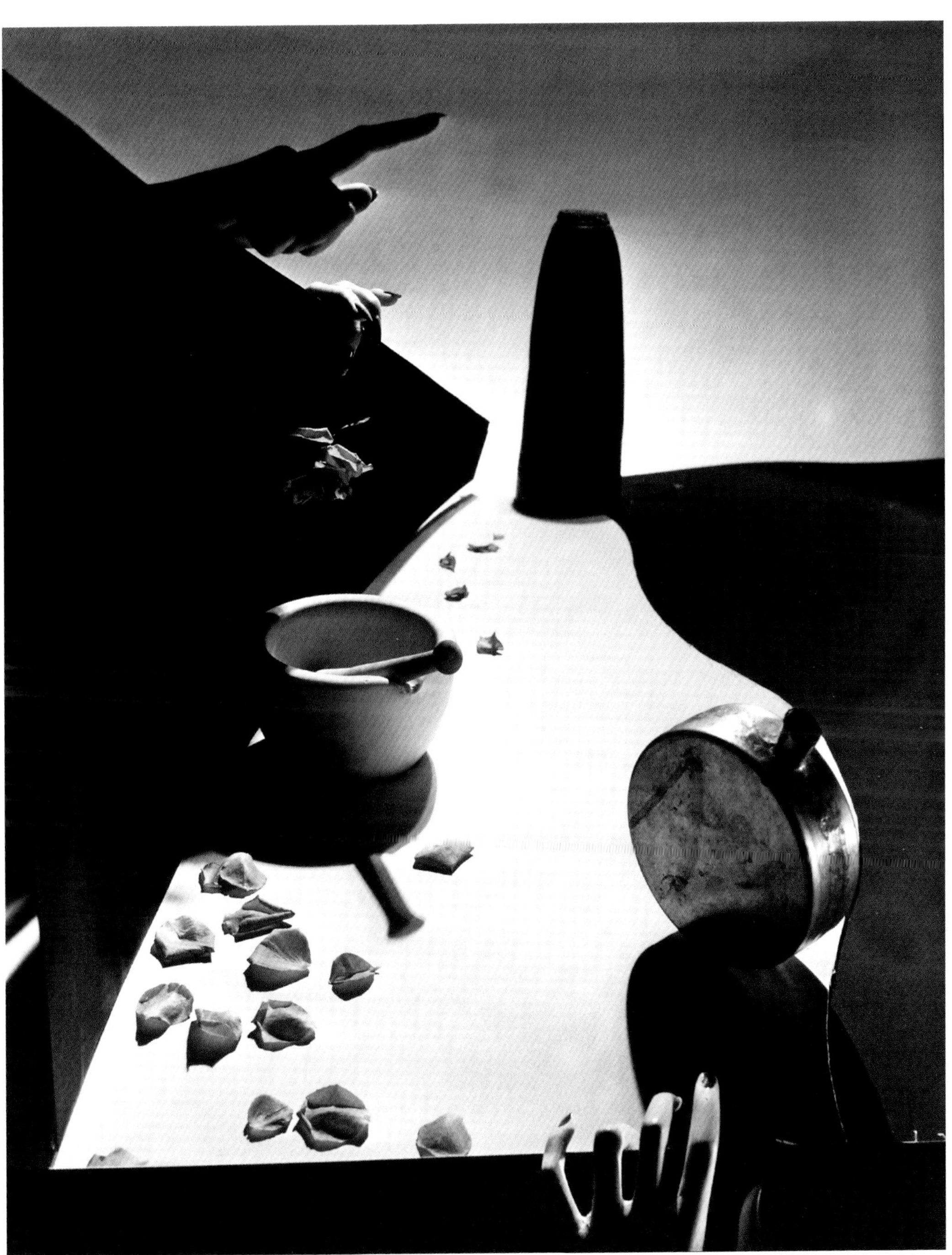

Surreal Beauty Cream, 1941

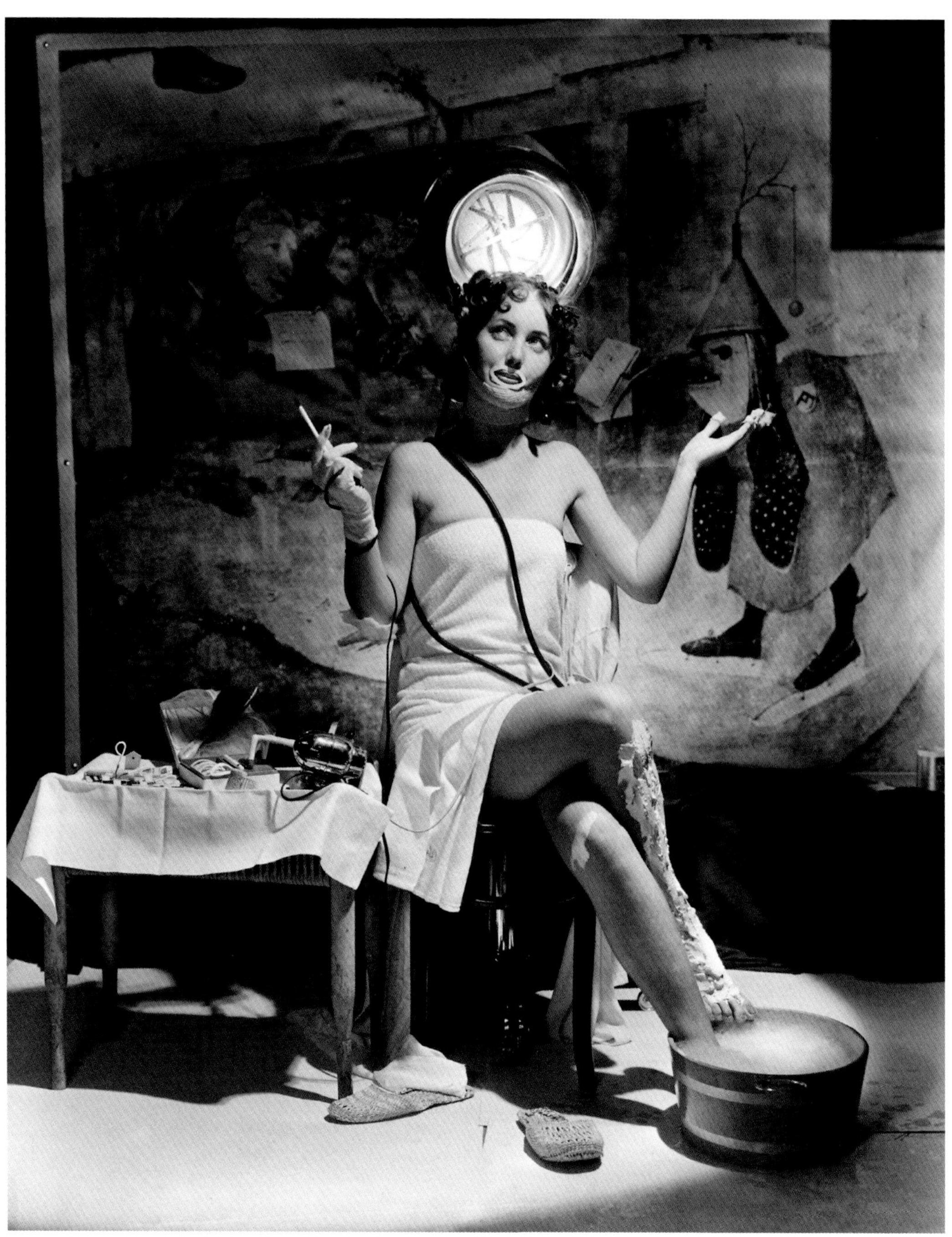

Electric Beauty, variant, 1939

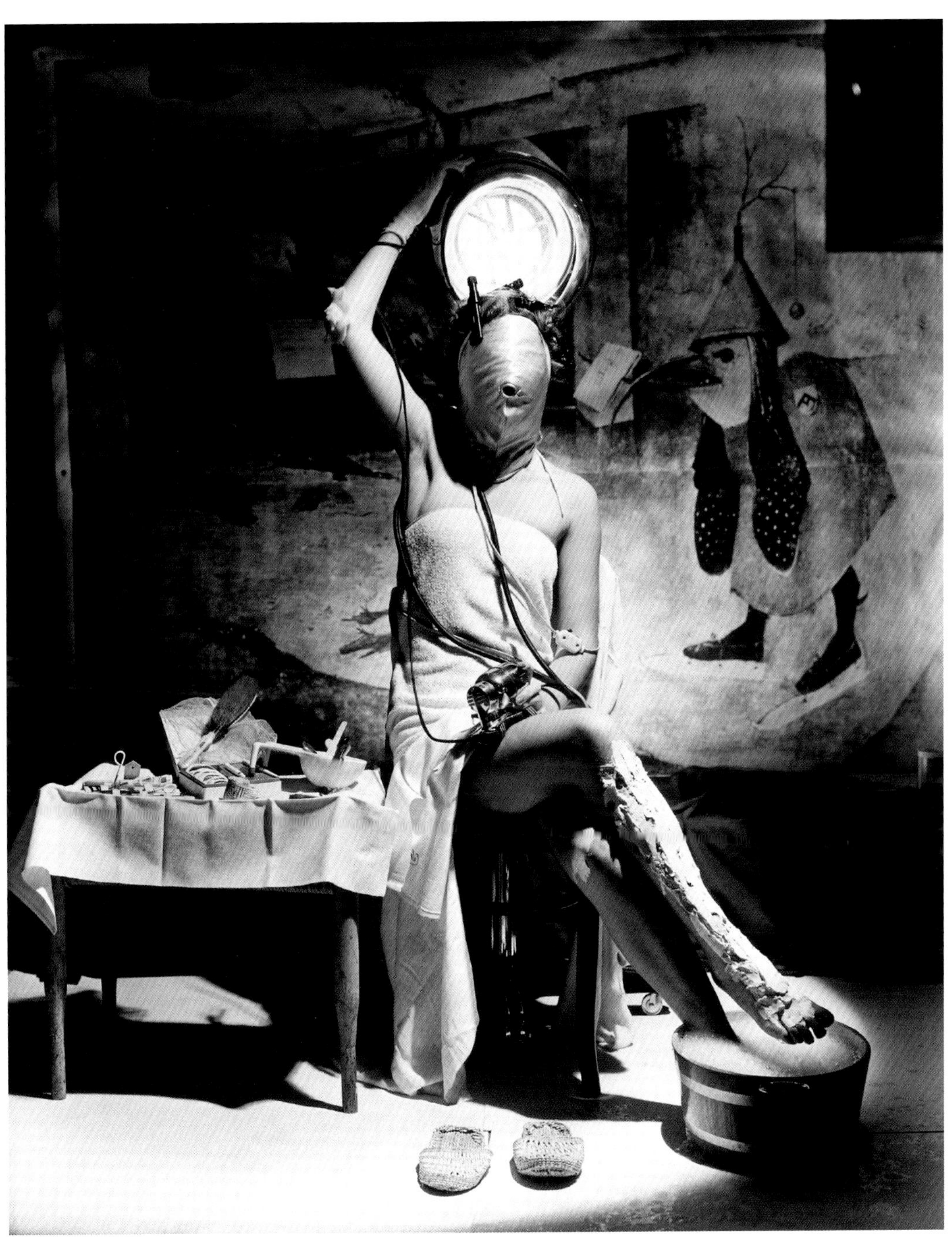

Electric Beauty, 1939

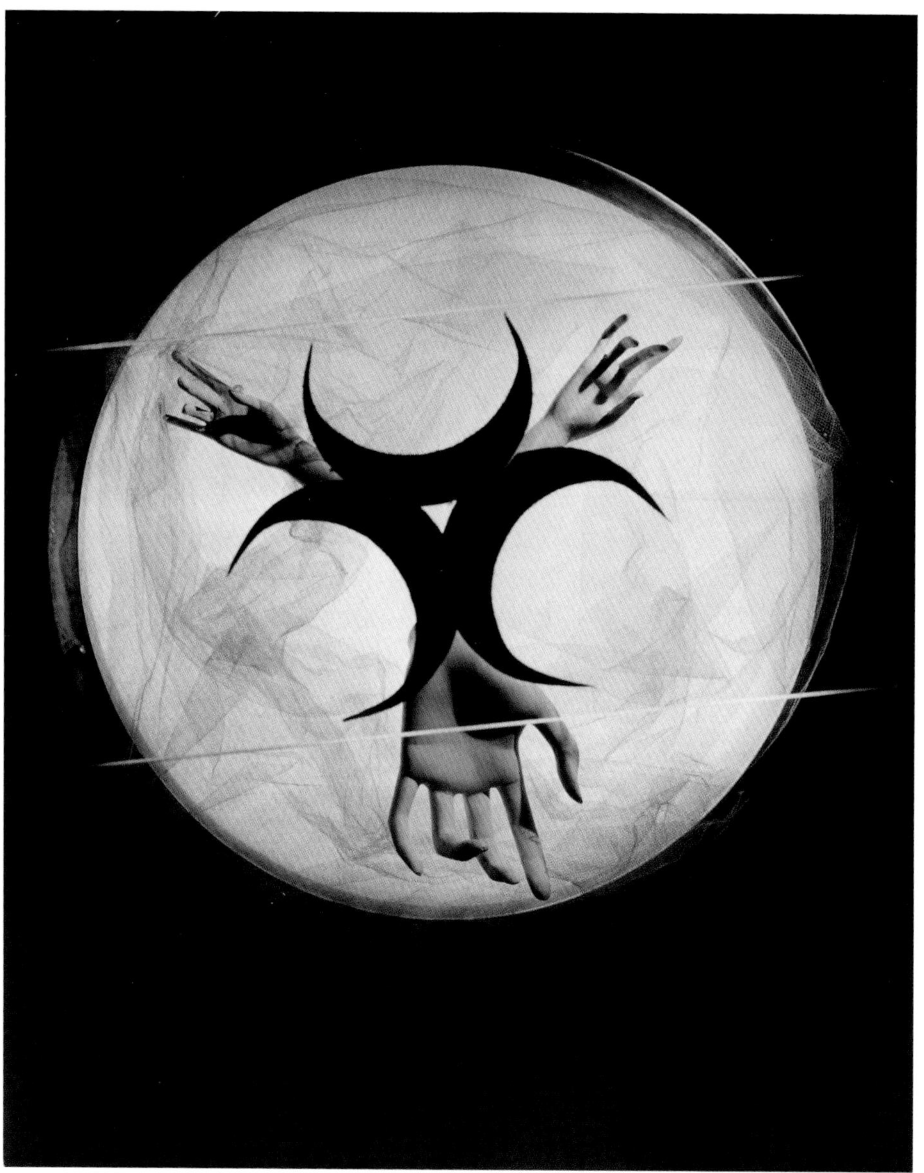

Surreal Composition, 1940

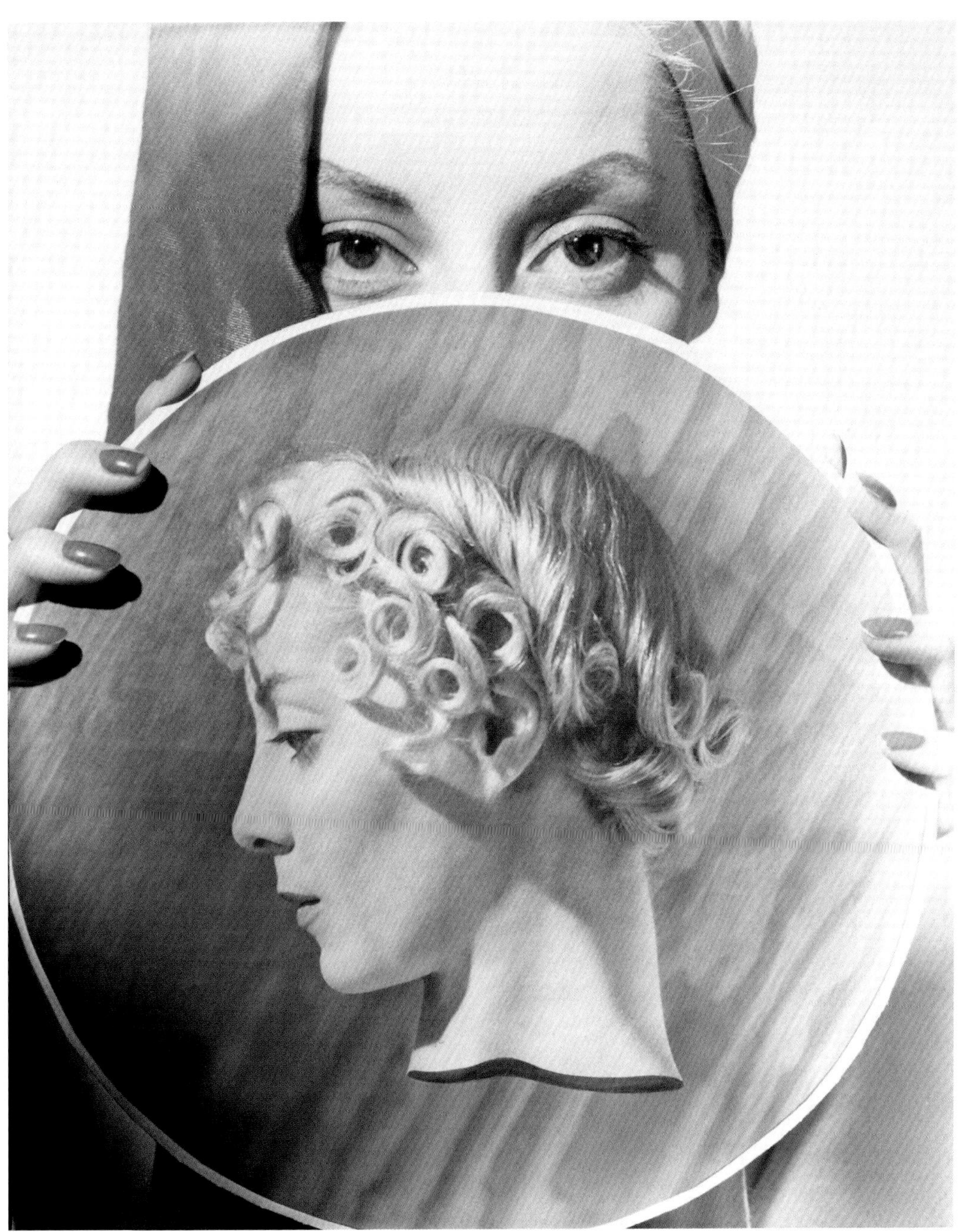

Helen Bennett, 1936

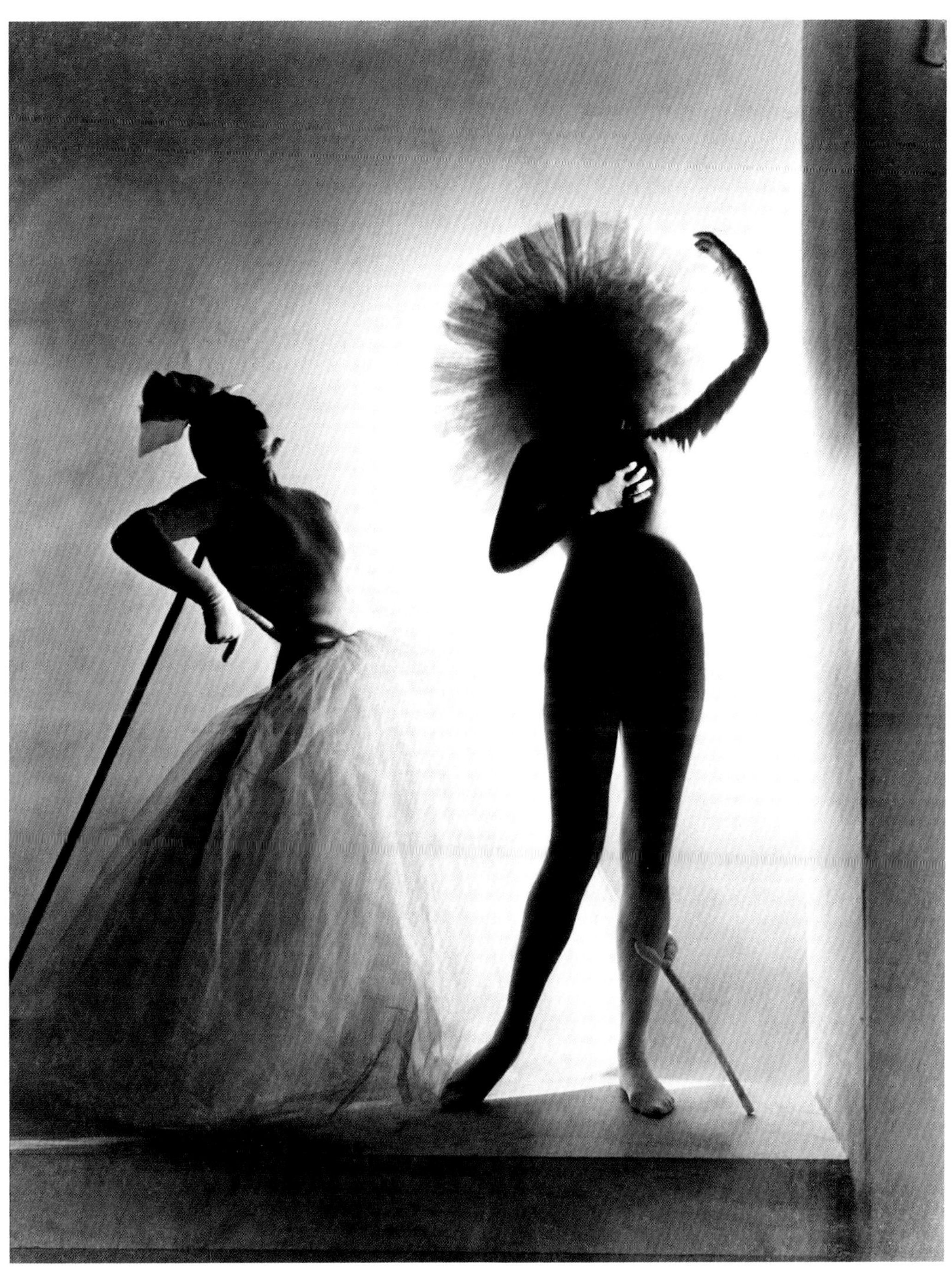

Costumes by Salvador Dalí, for Leonid Massine's ballet, *Bacchanale*, 1939

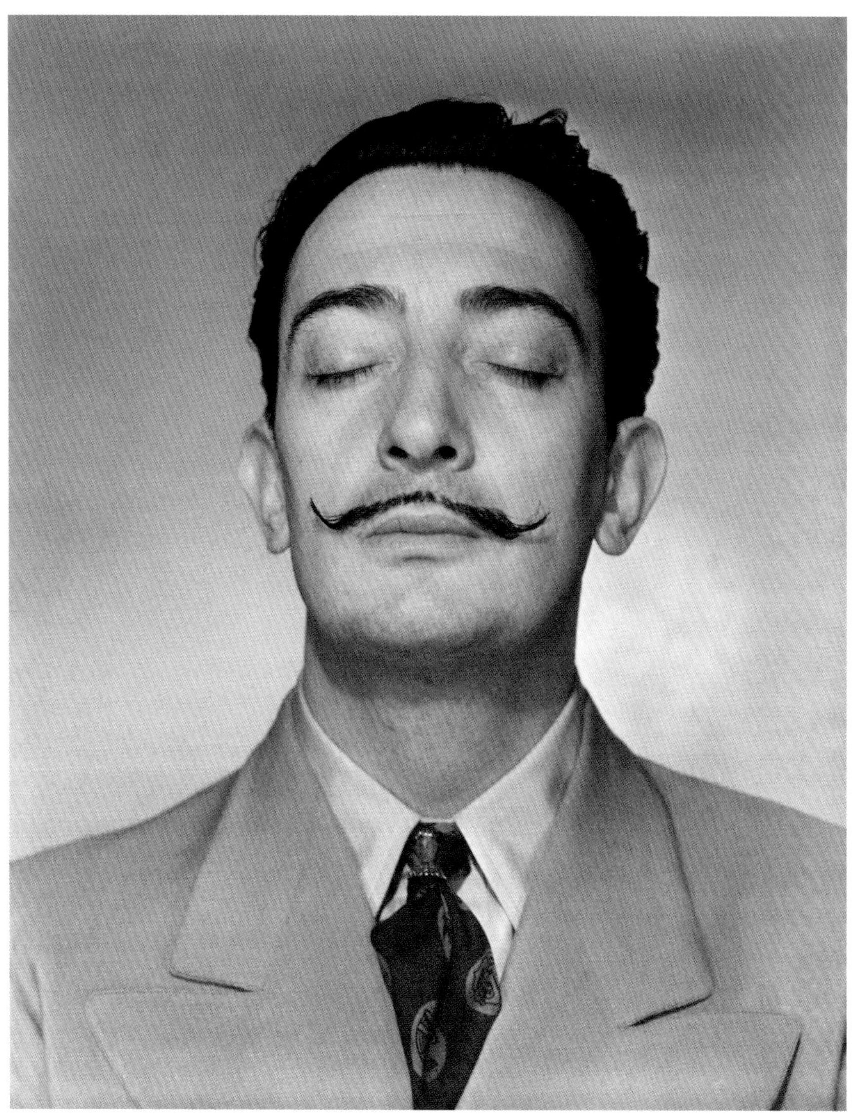

Salvador Dalí, New York, 1943

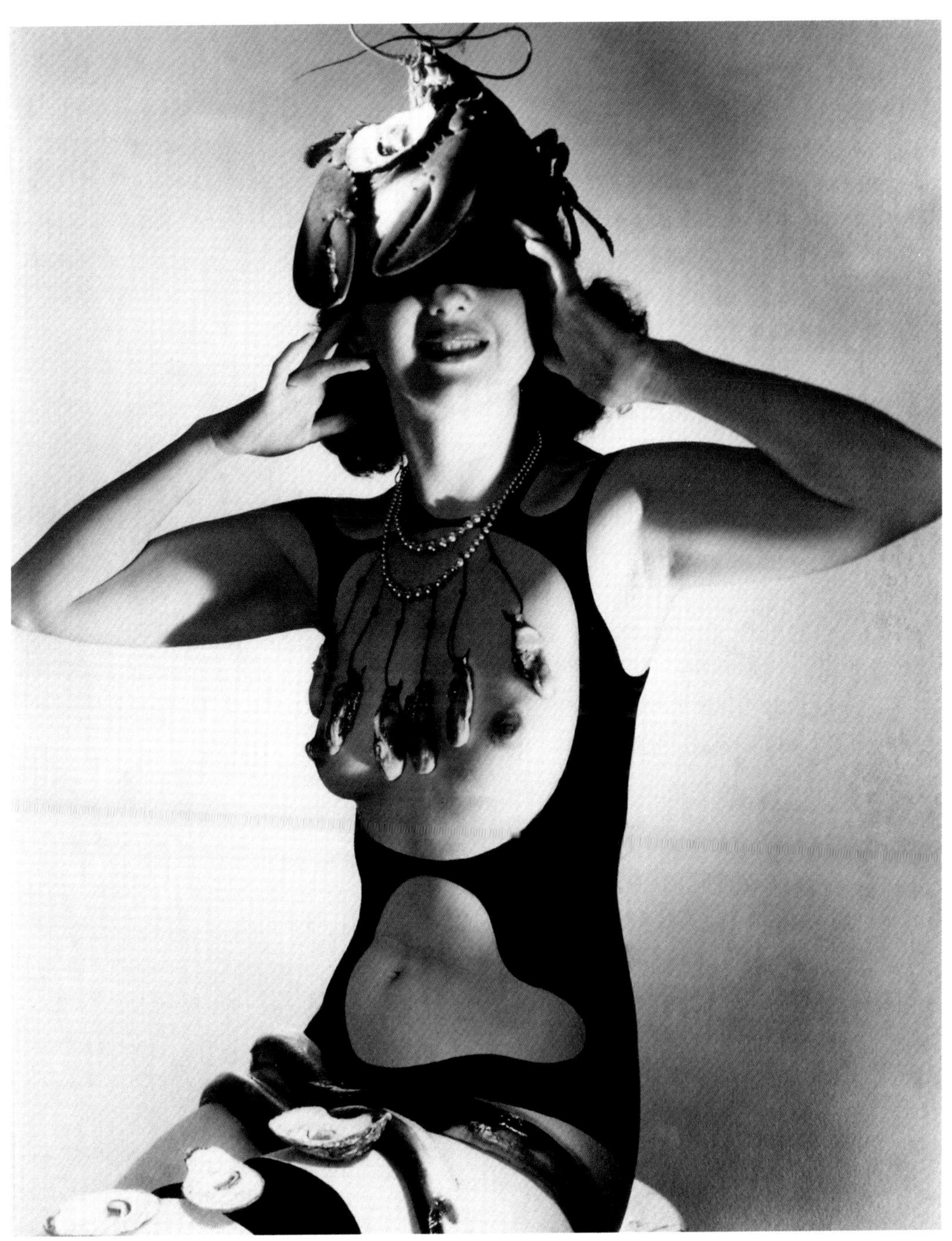

Costume for Salvador Dalí's *Dream of Venus*, 1939

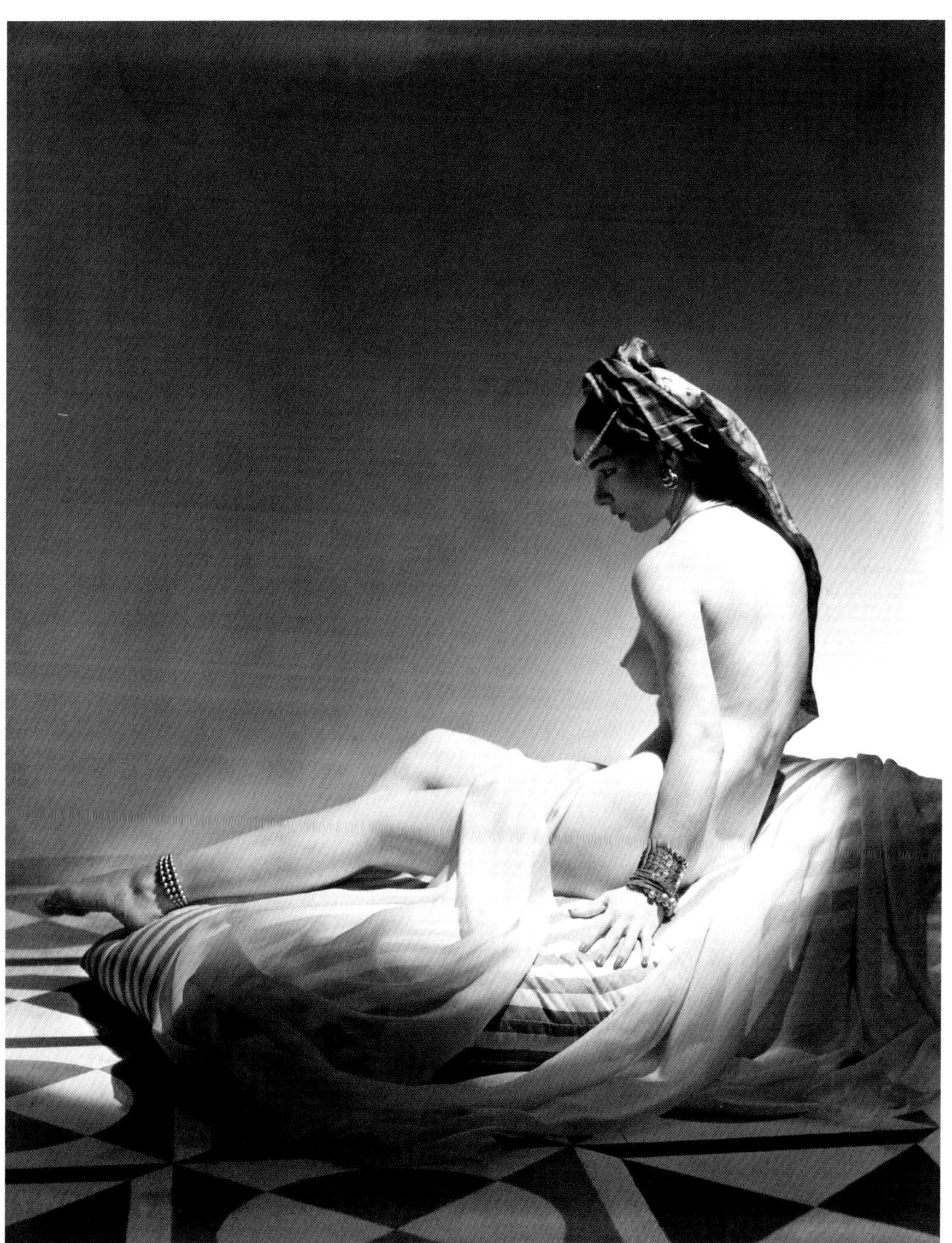

Odalisque, 1943

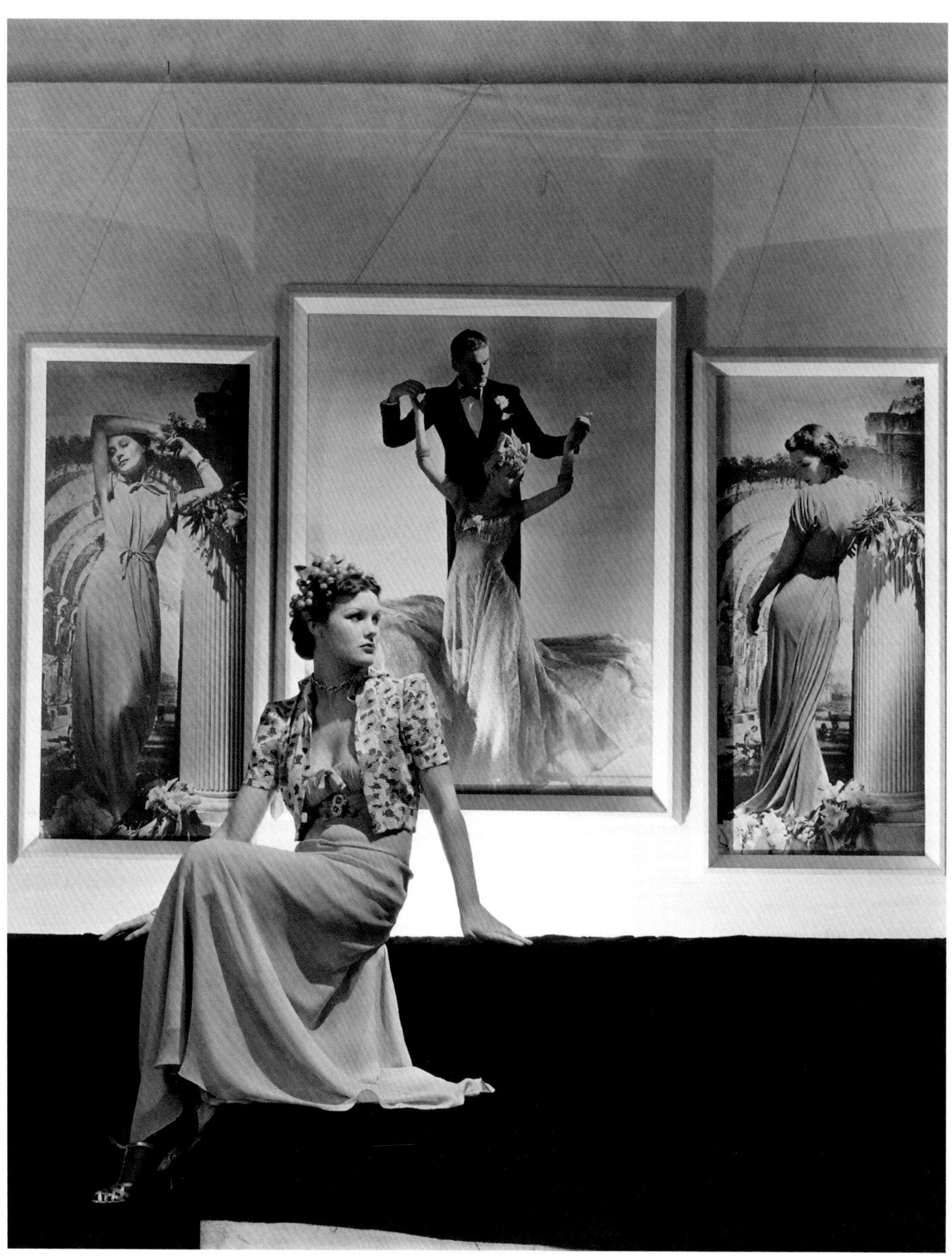

Dress by Milgram, jewellery by Black, Starr and Frost-Gorham, 1938

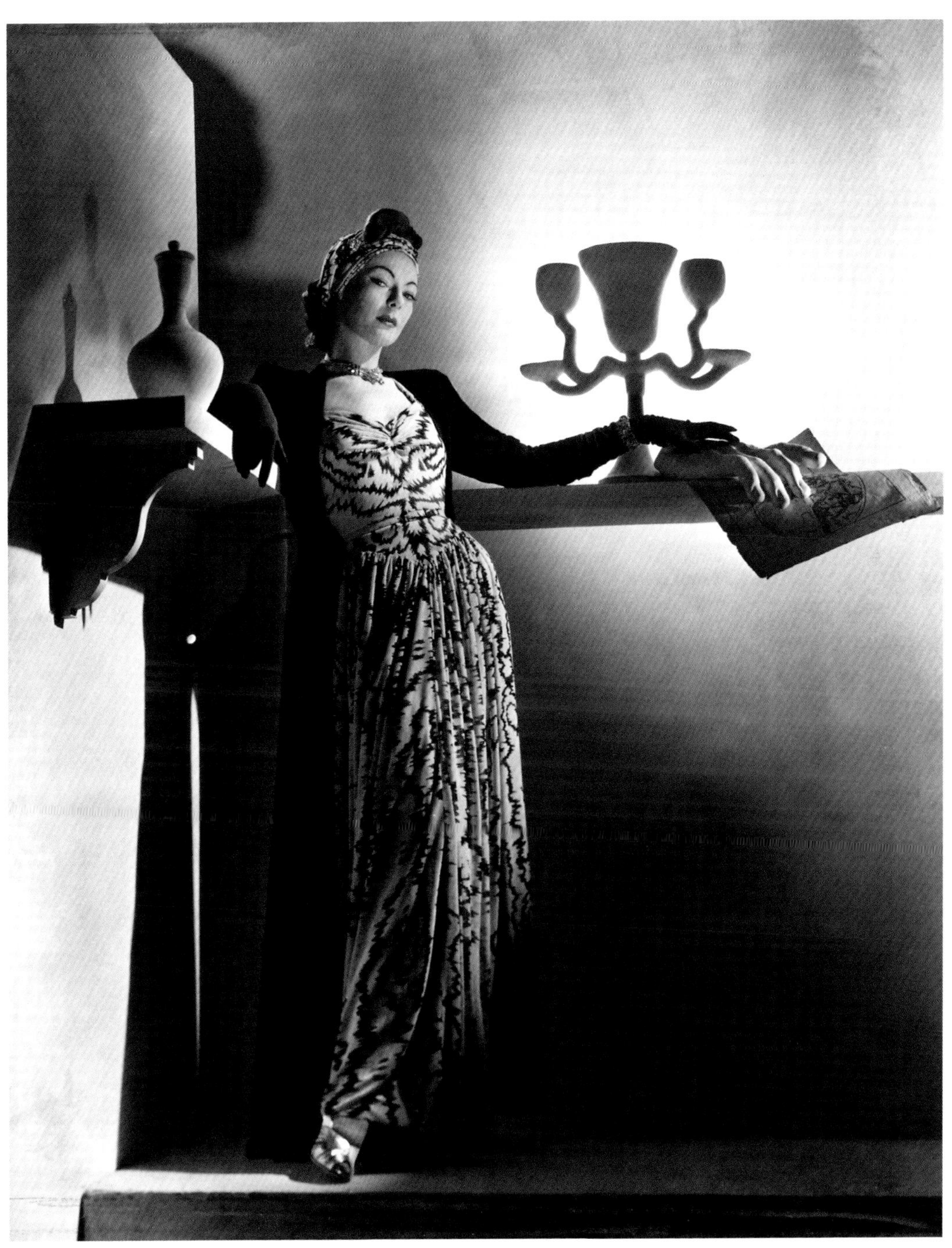

Dress by Nettie Rosenstein, jewellery by Trabert and Hoeffer-Mauboussin, Tutankhamun lamp by Alberto Giacometti

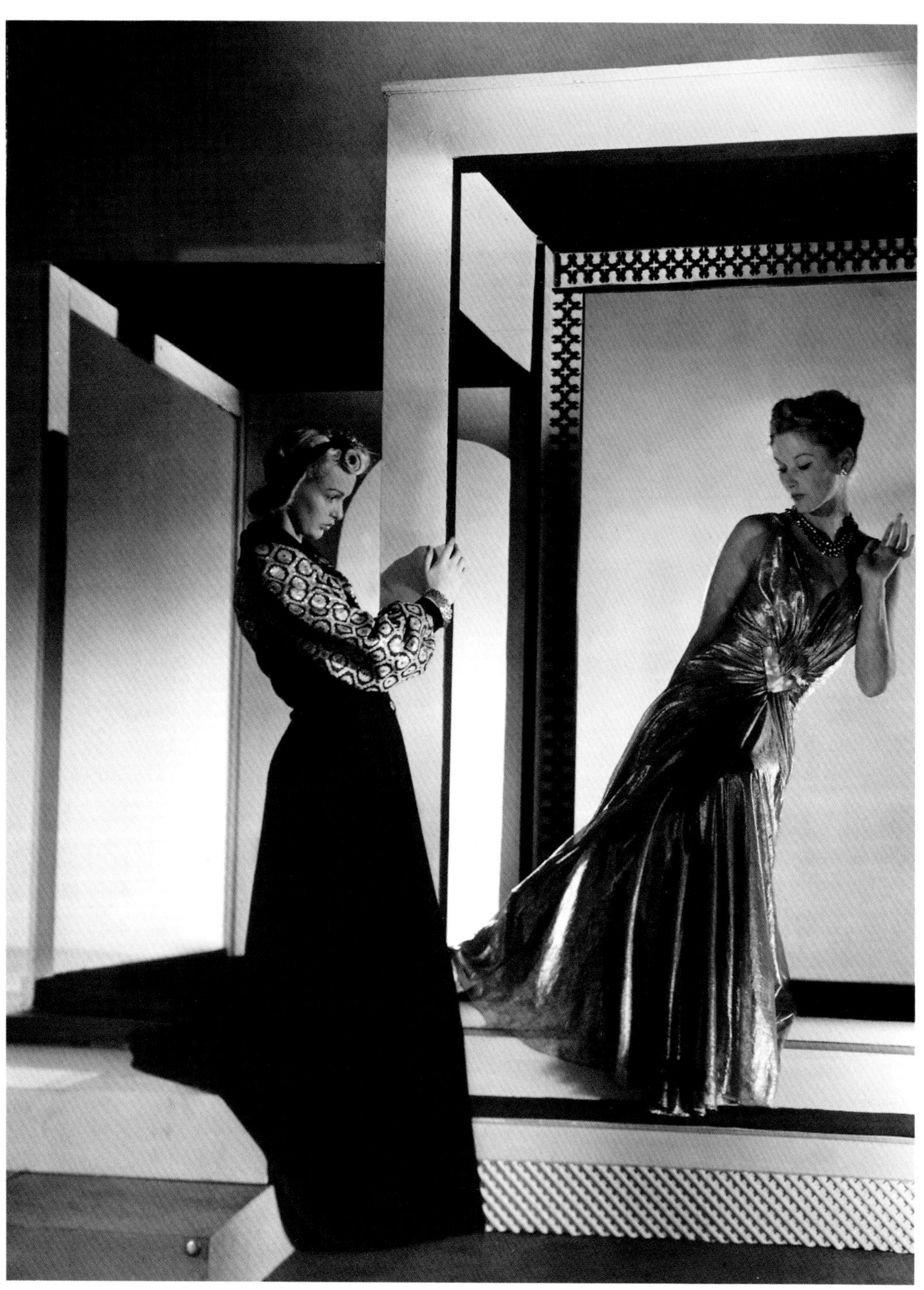

Madame Buchardt and Lisa Fonssagrives, evening coat and dress by Lucien Lelong, 1938

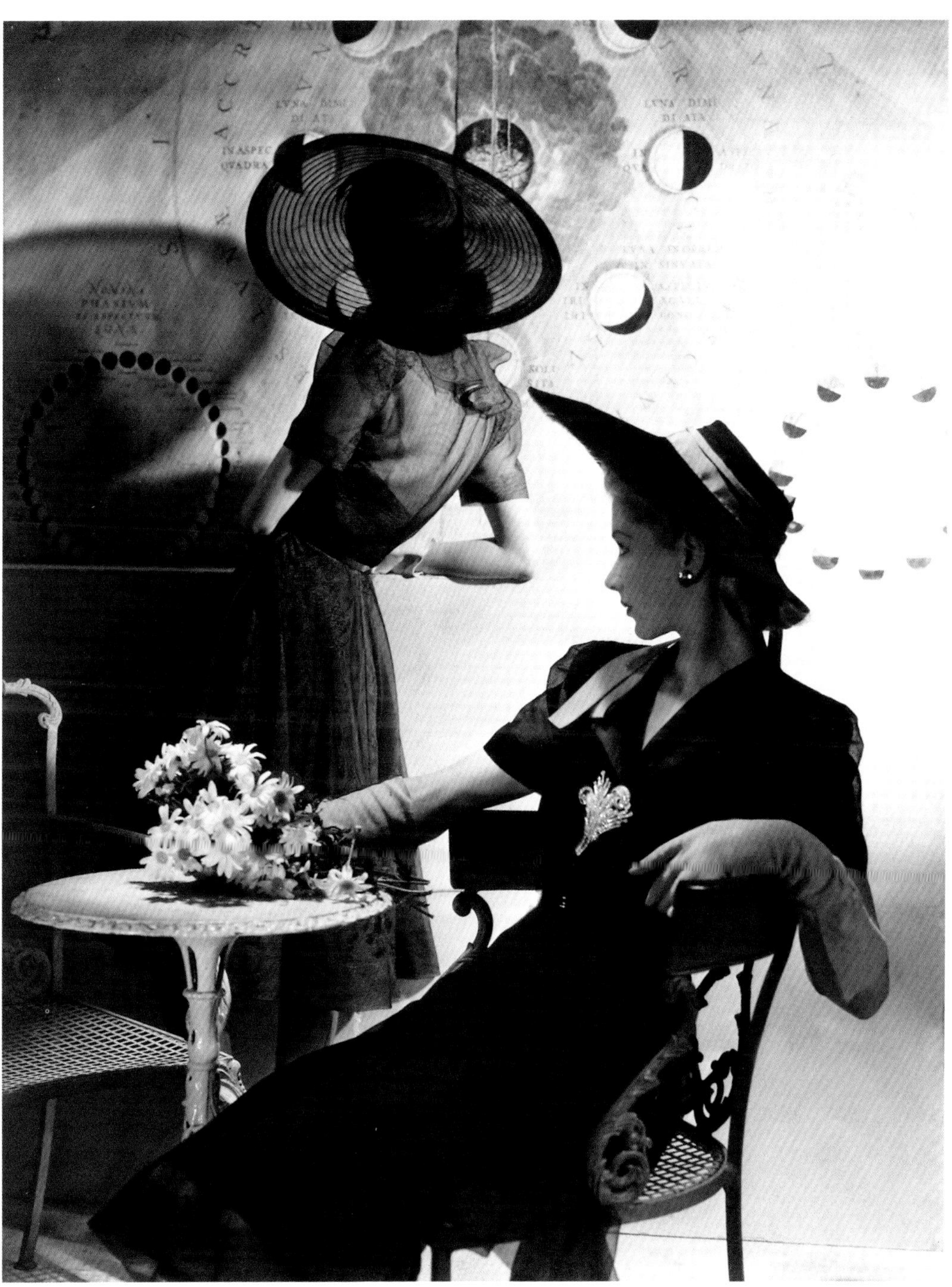

Miss Lane and Lisa Fonssagrives, dresses and hats by Saks-Fifth Avenue, 1940

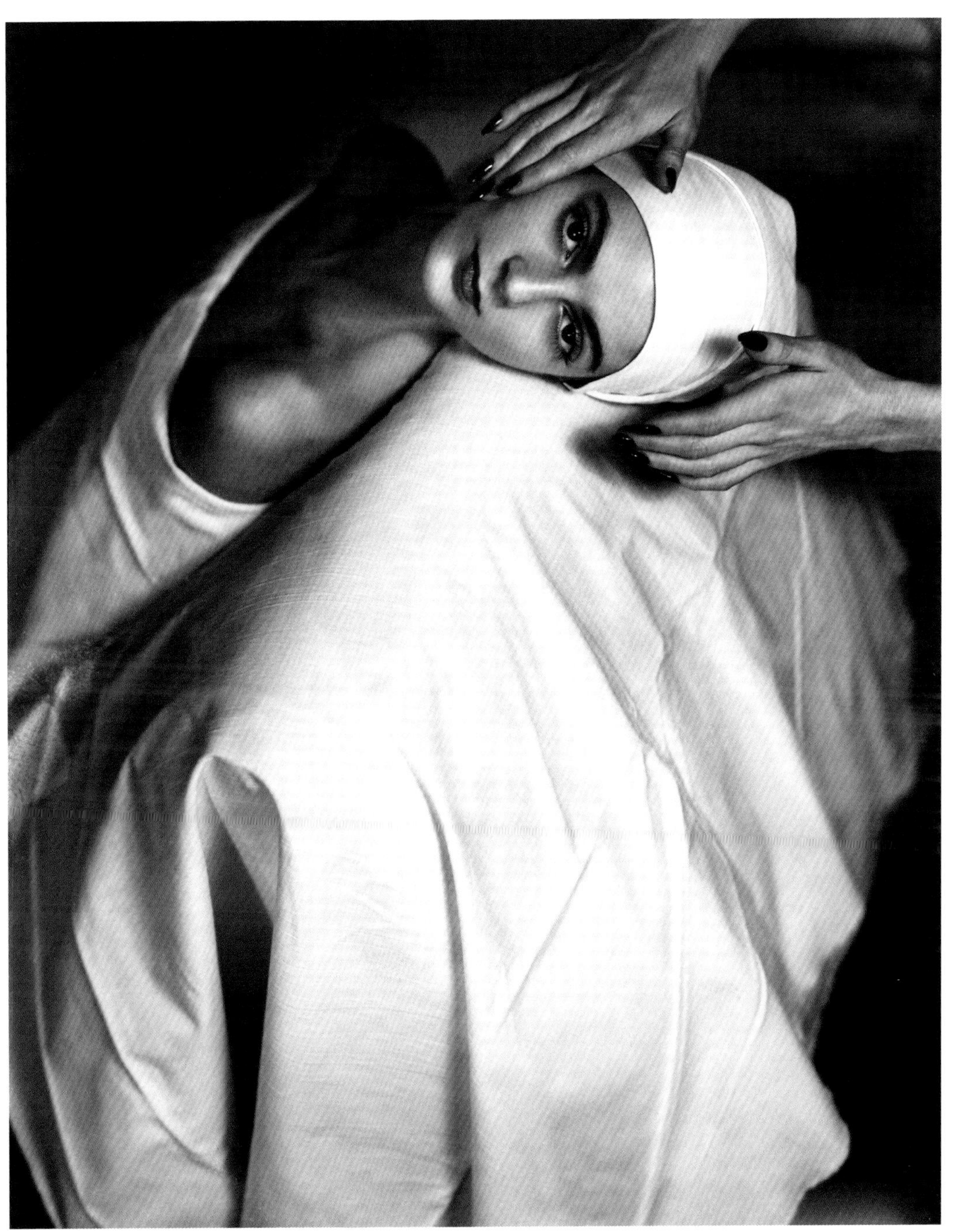

Carmen Dell'Orefice, *Carmen Face Massage*, 1946

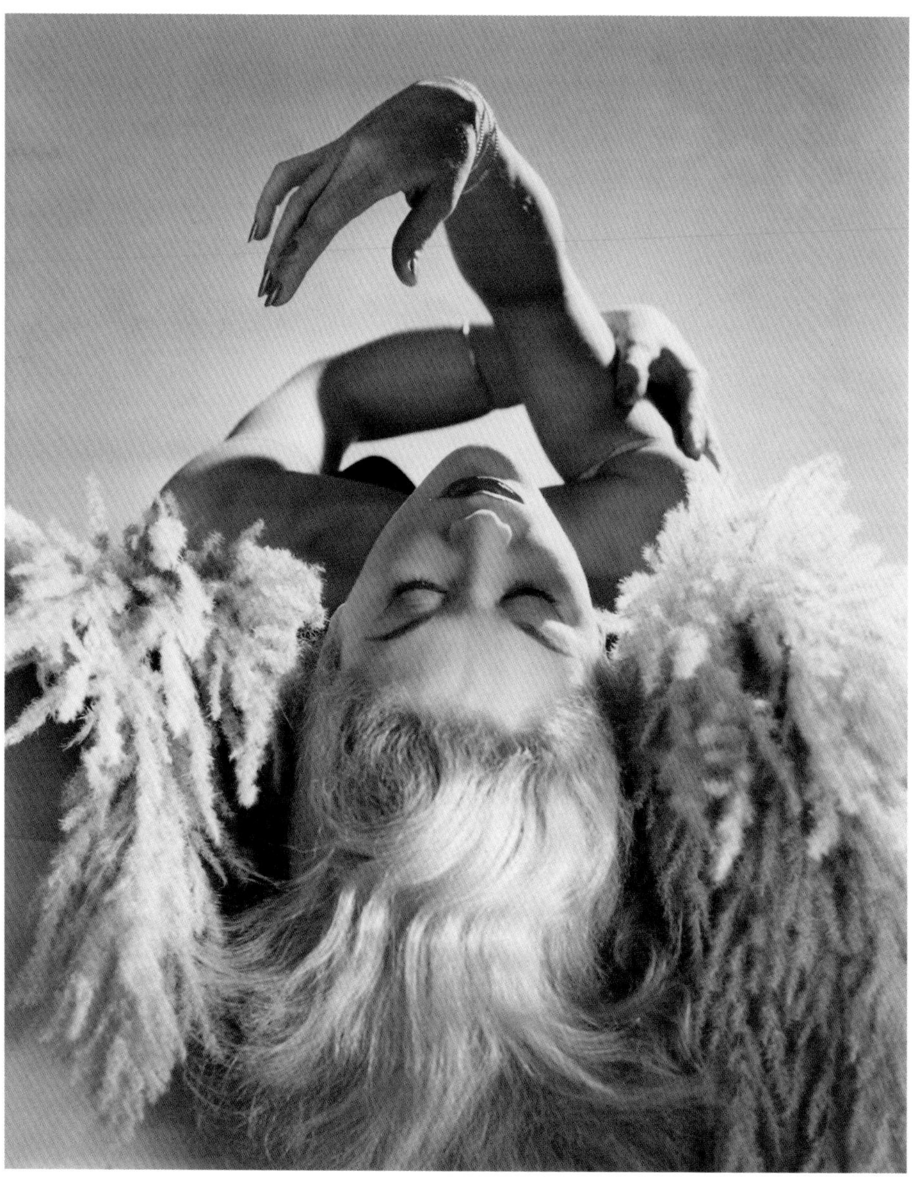

Lisa Fonssagrives, *Hair*, 1939

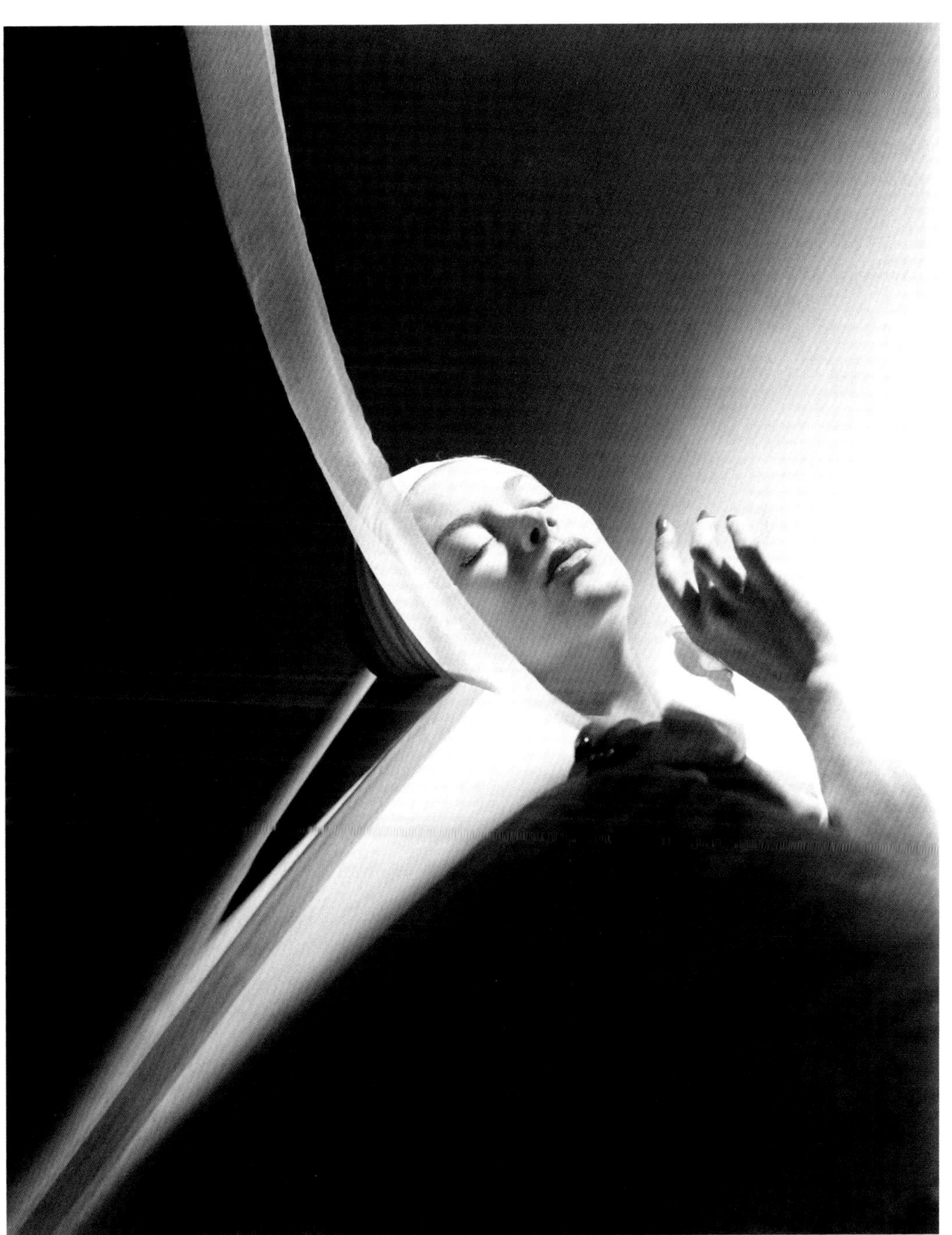

Lisa Fonssagrives, *Lisa with Turban*, 1940

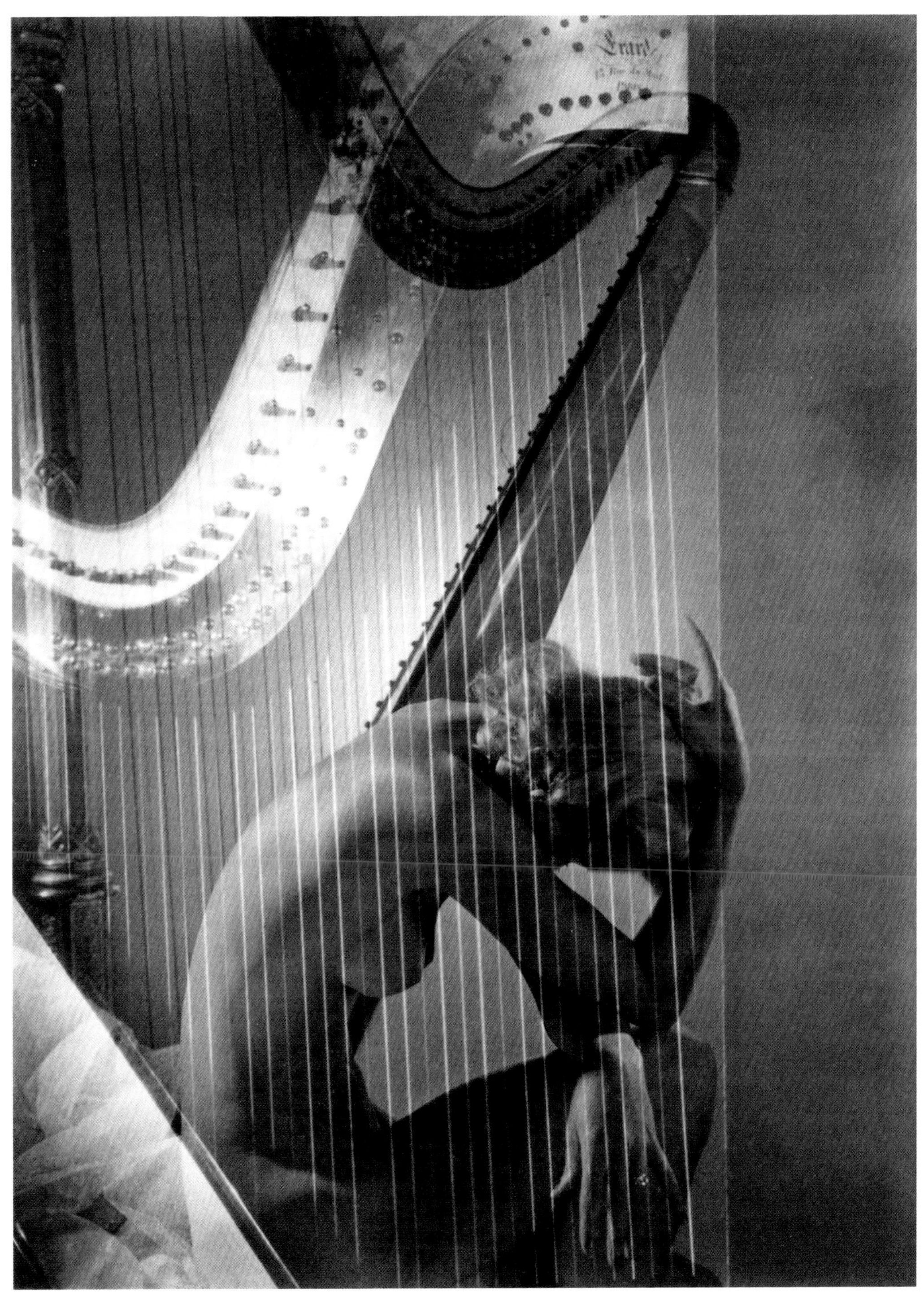

Lisa Fonssagrives, *Lisa with Harp*, 1939

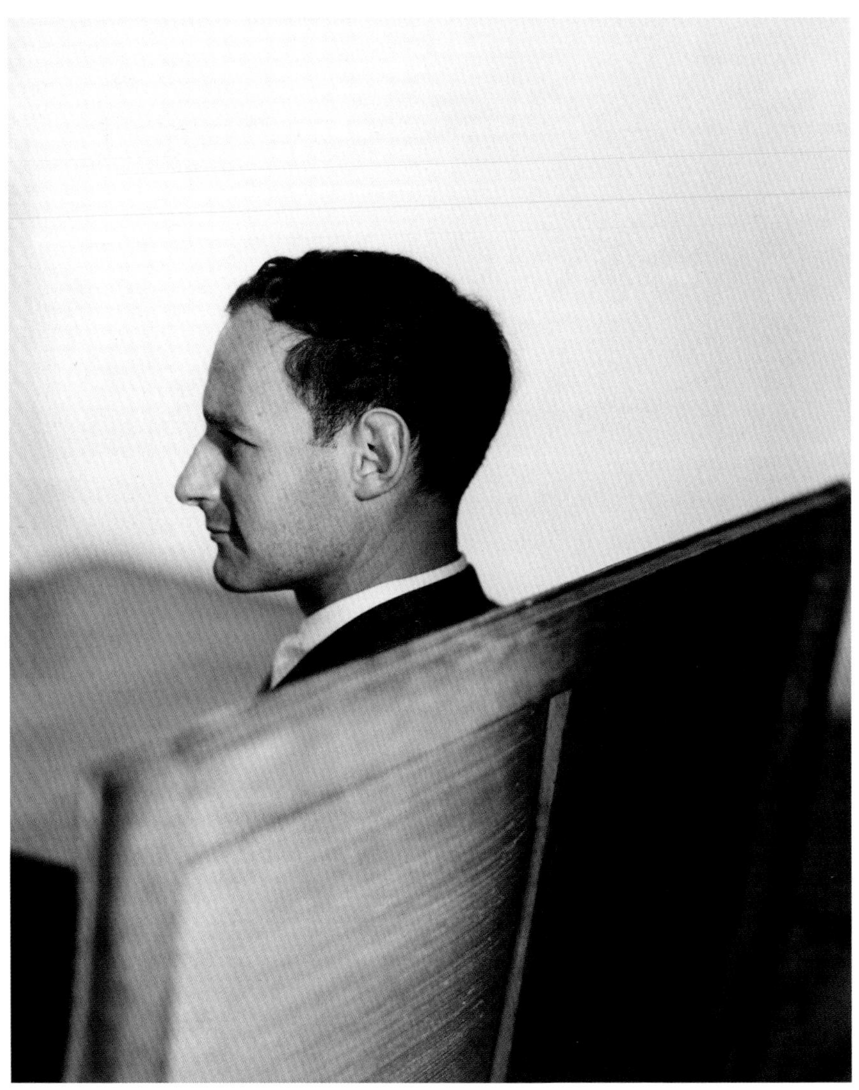

Irving Penn, New York, 1951

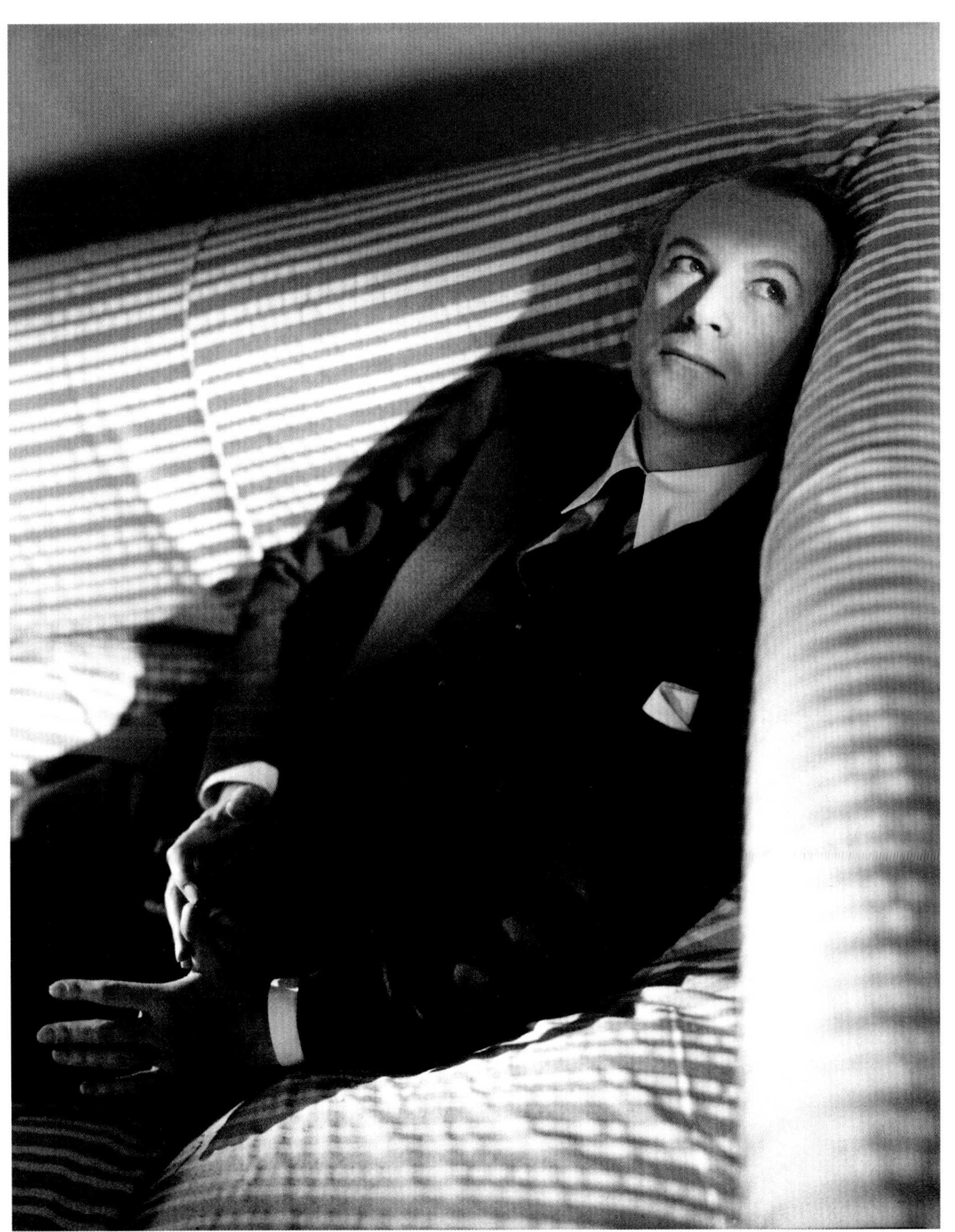

Cecil Beaton, Paris, 1934

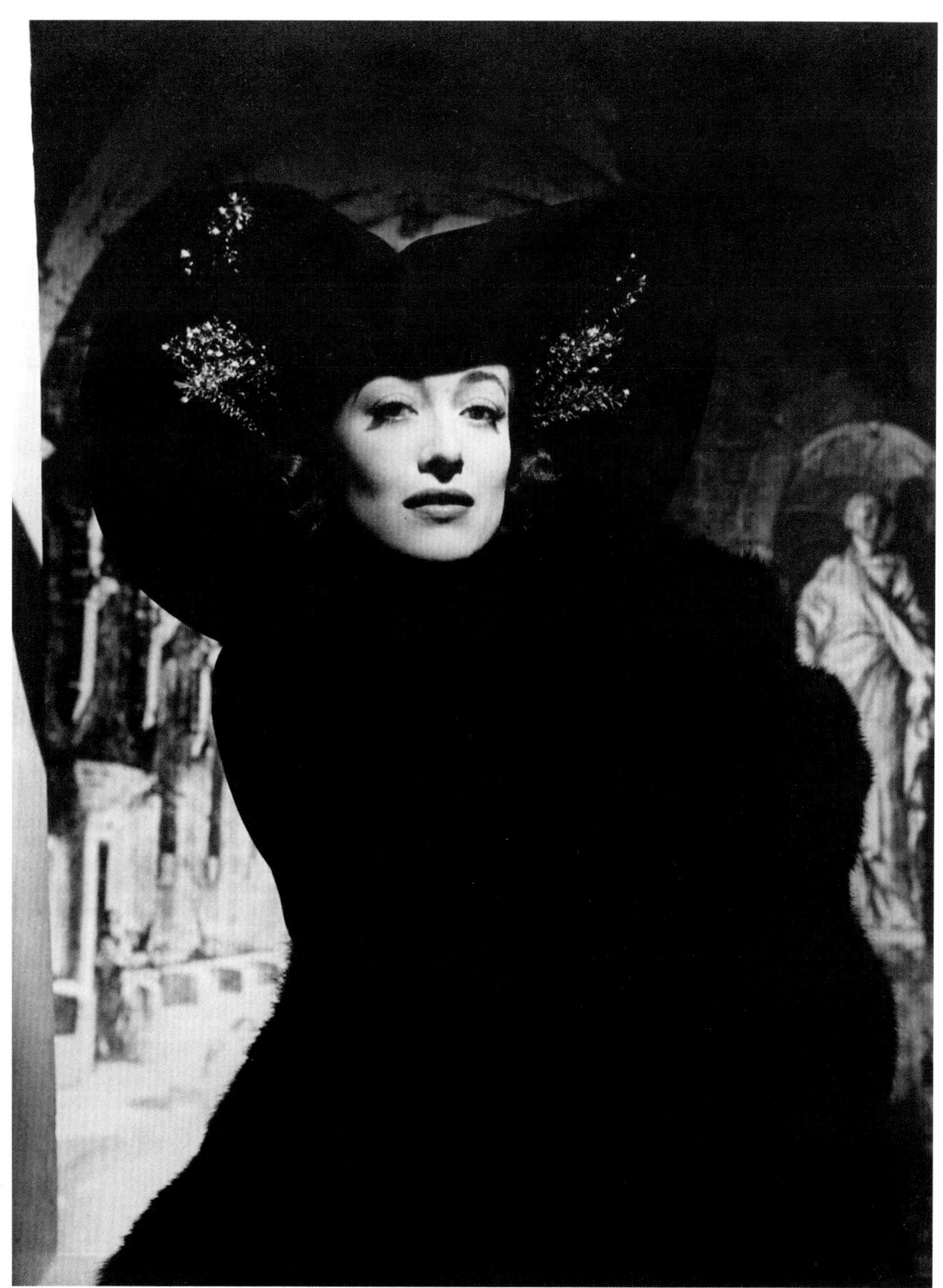

Joan Crawford, New York, 1938

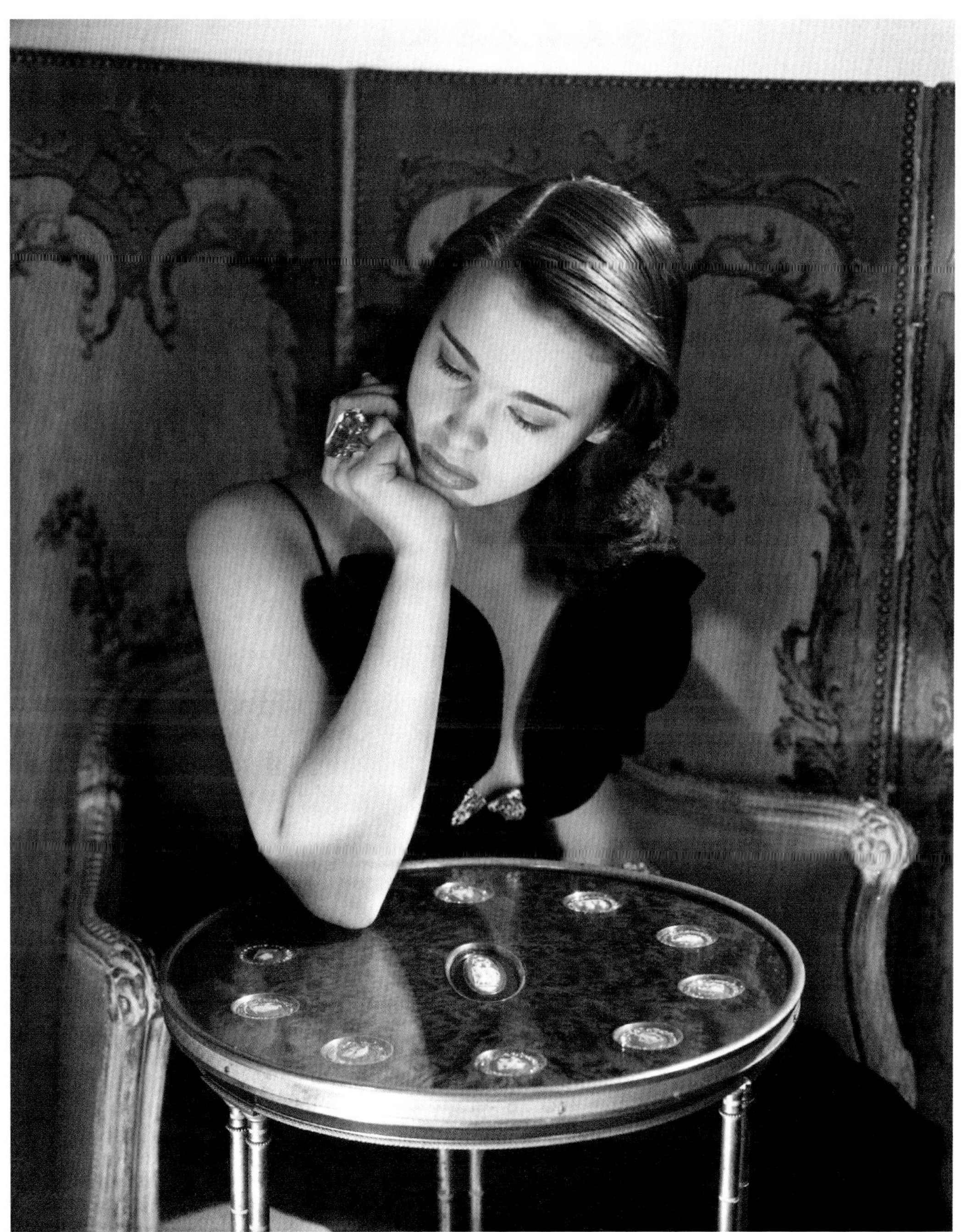

Gloria Vanderbilt, New York, 1941

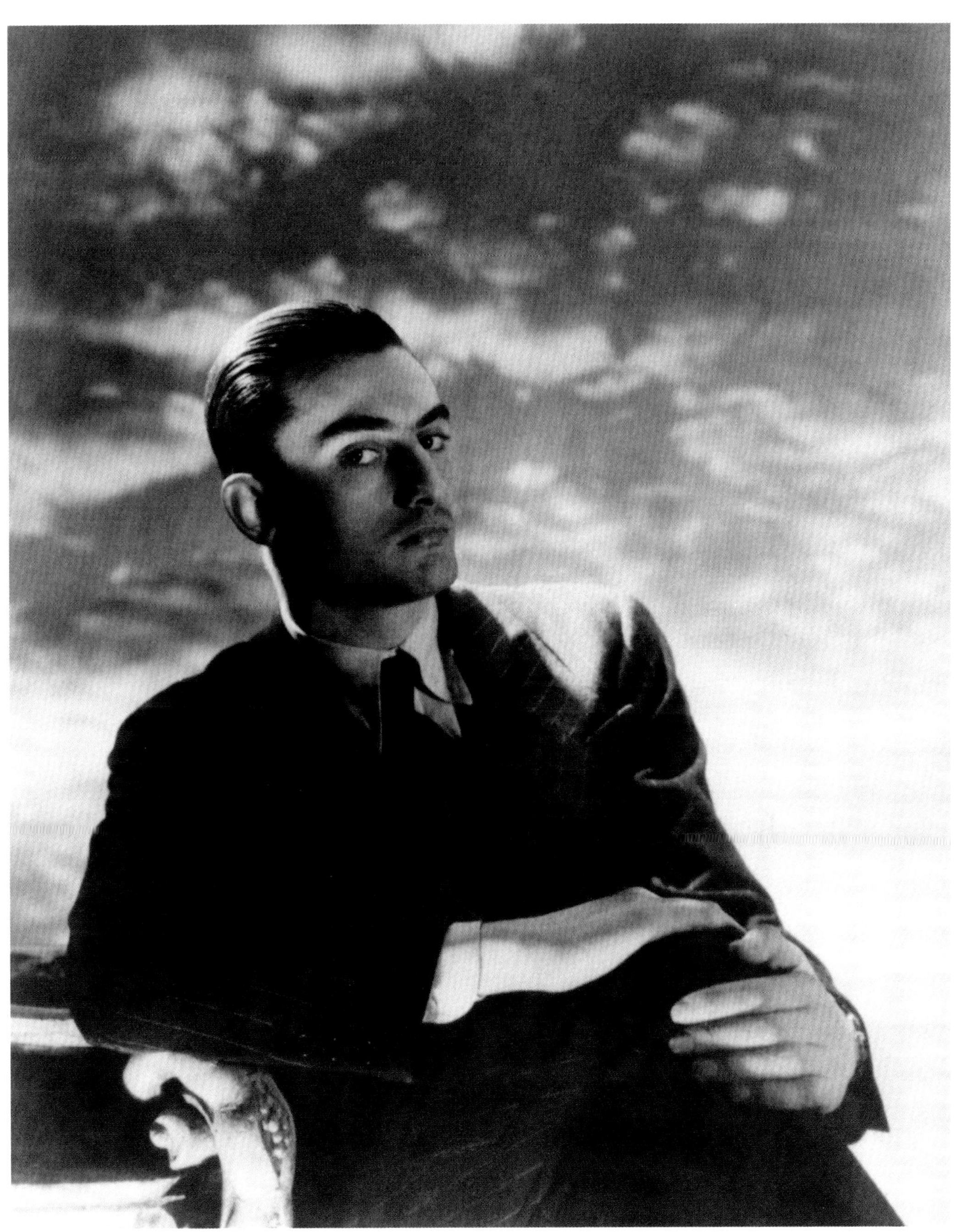

Luchino Visconti, Paris, 1937

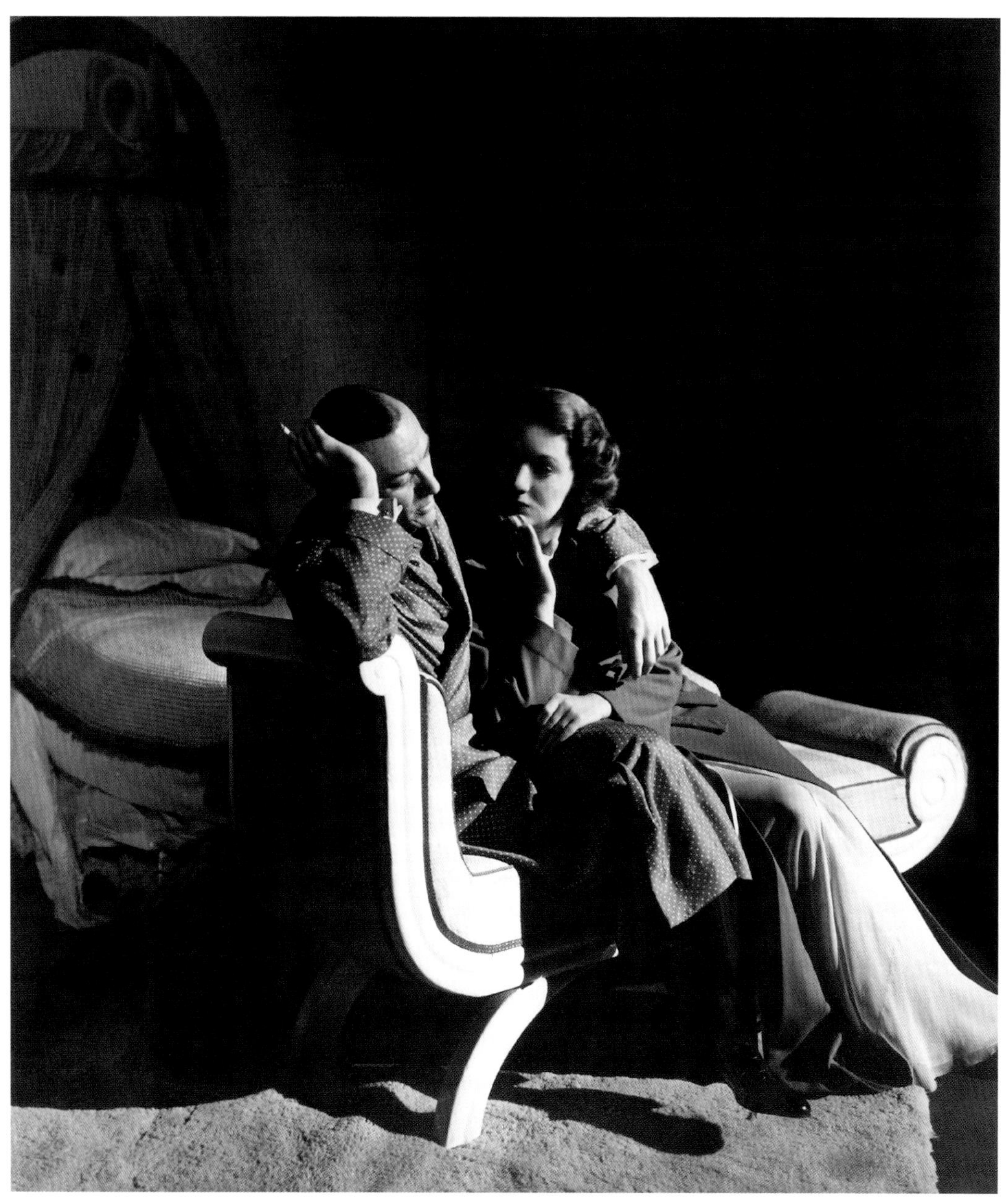

Noël Coward and Gertrude Lawrence on the set of *Tonight at 8:30*, Boston, 1936

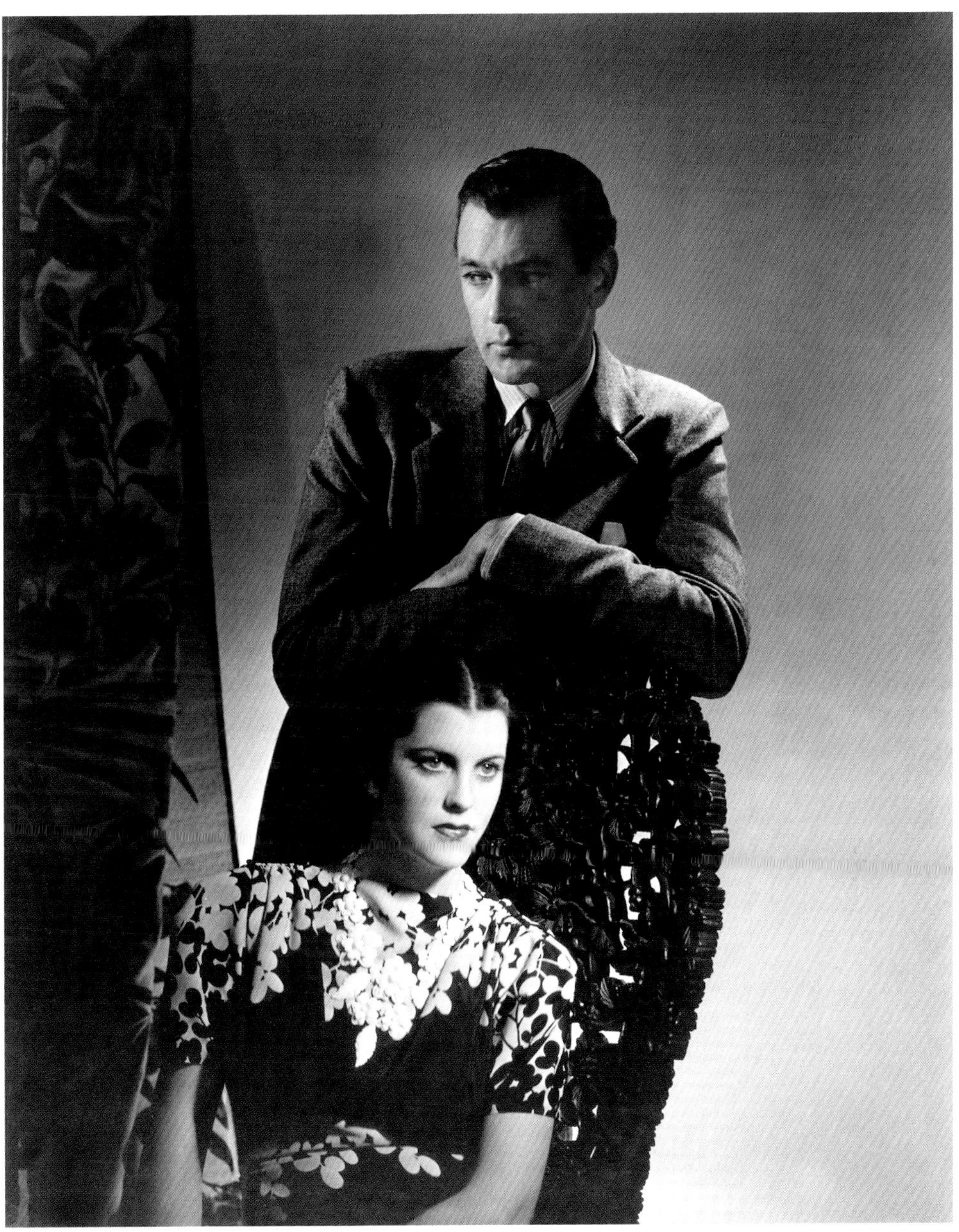

Gary Cooper and his wife Rocky, New York, 1938

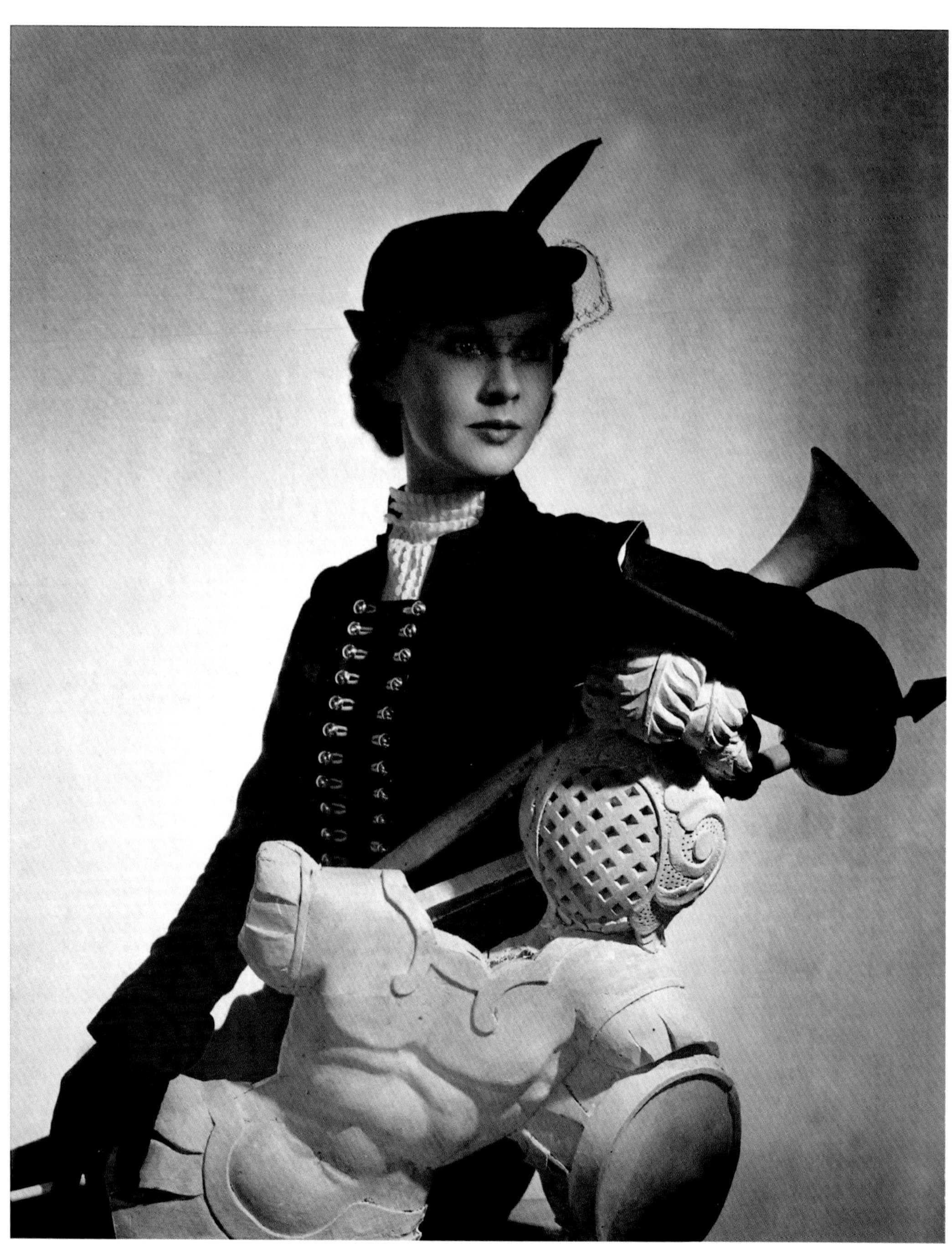

Vivien Leigh, London, 1936

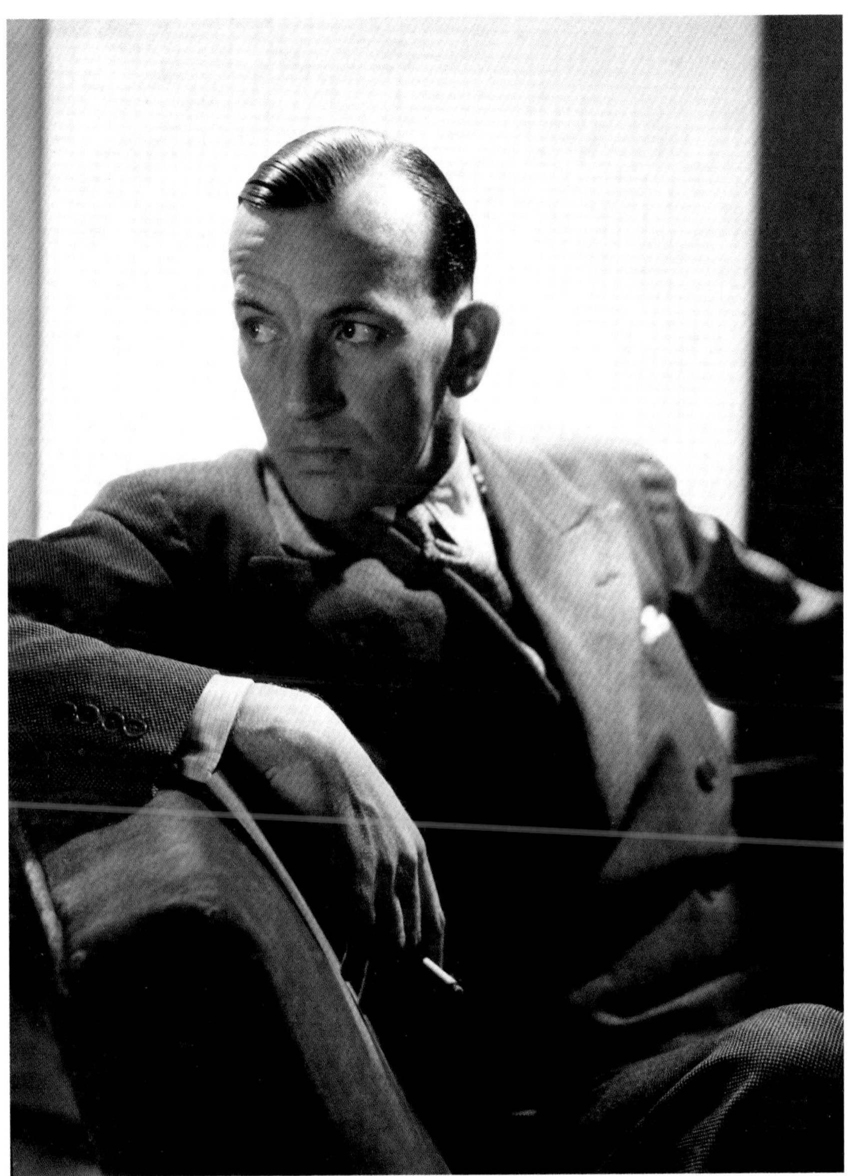

Noël Coward, London, 1933

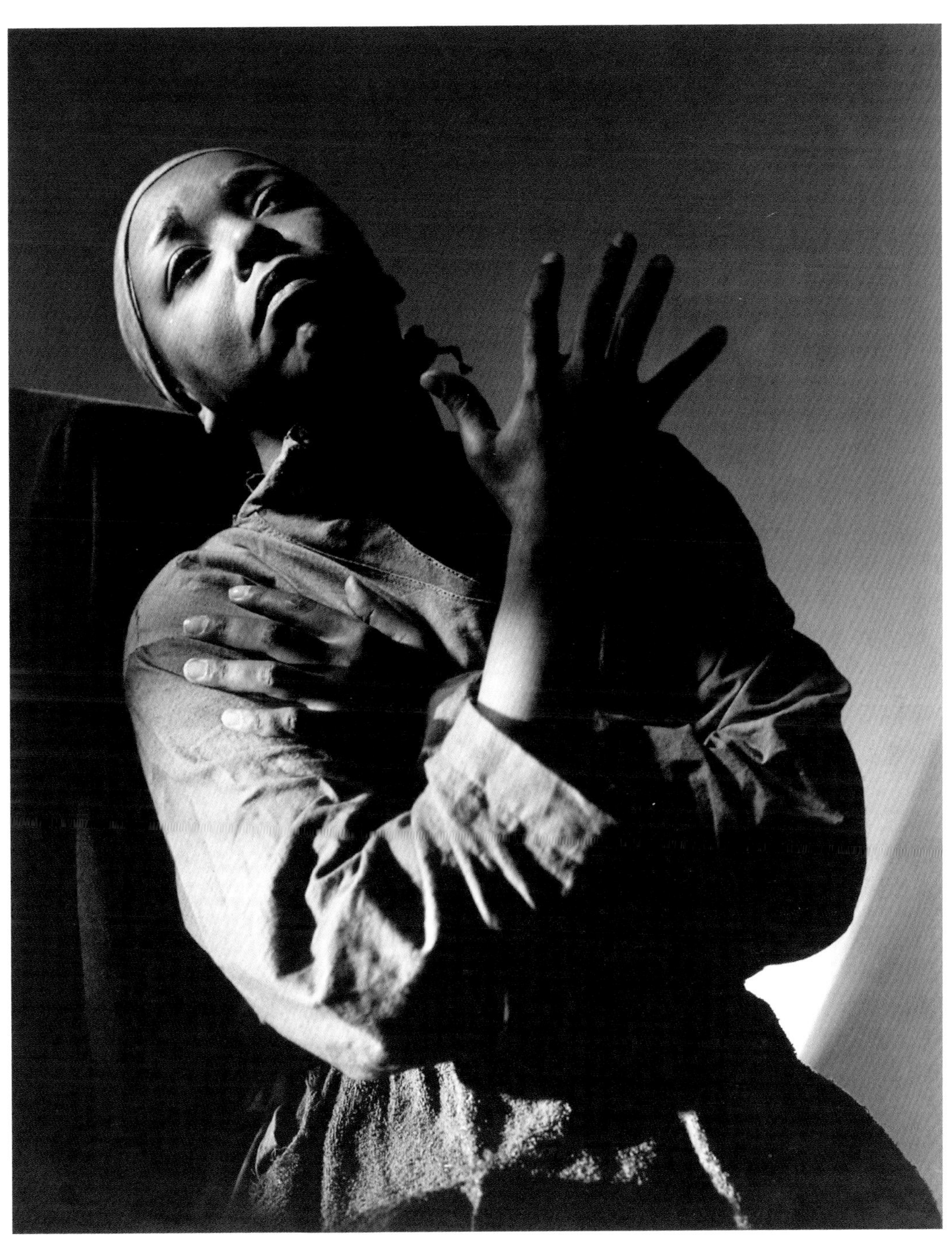

Ethel Waters as Hagar in *Mamba's Daughters*, New York, 1939

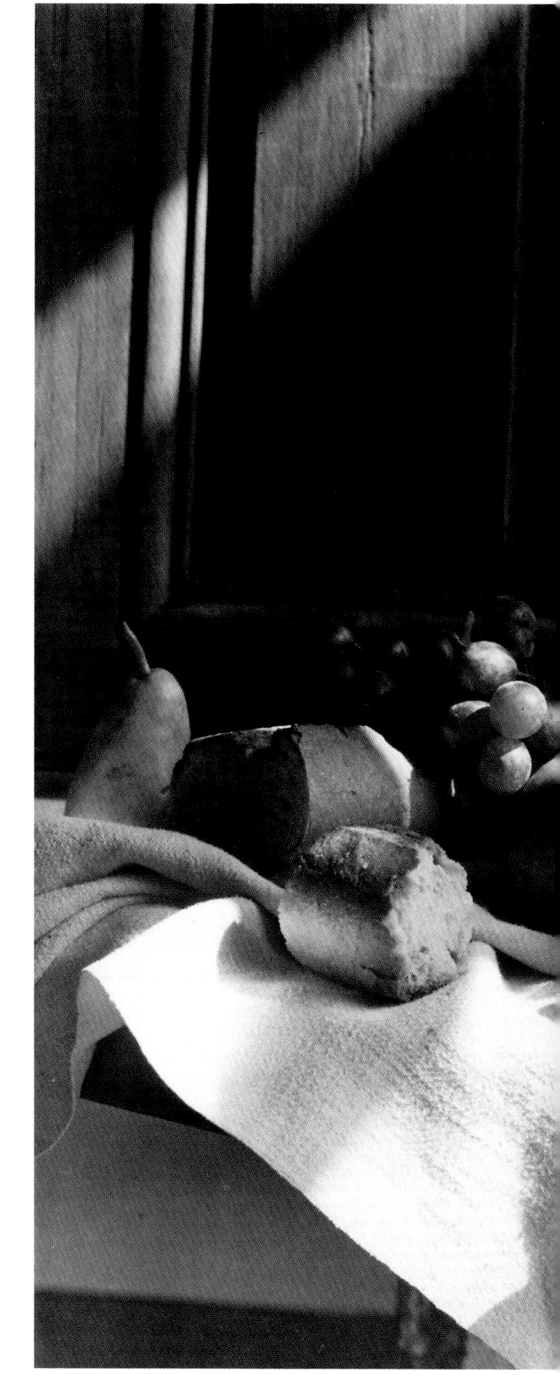

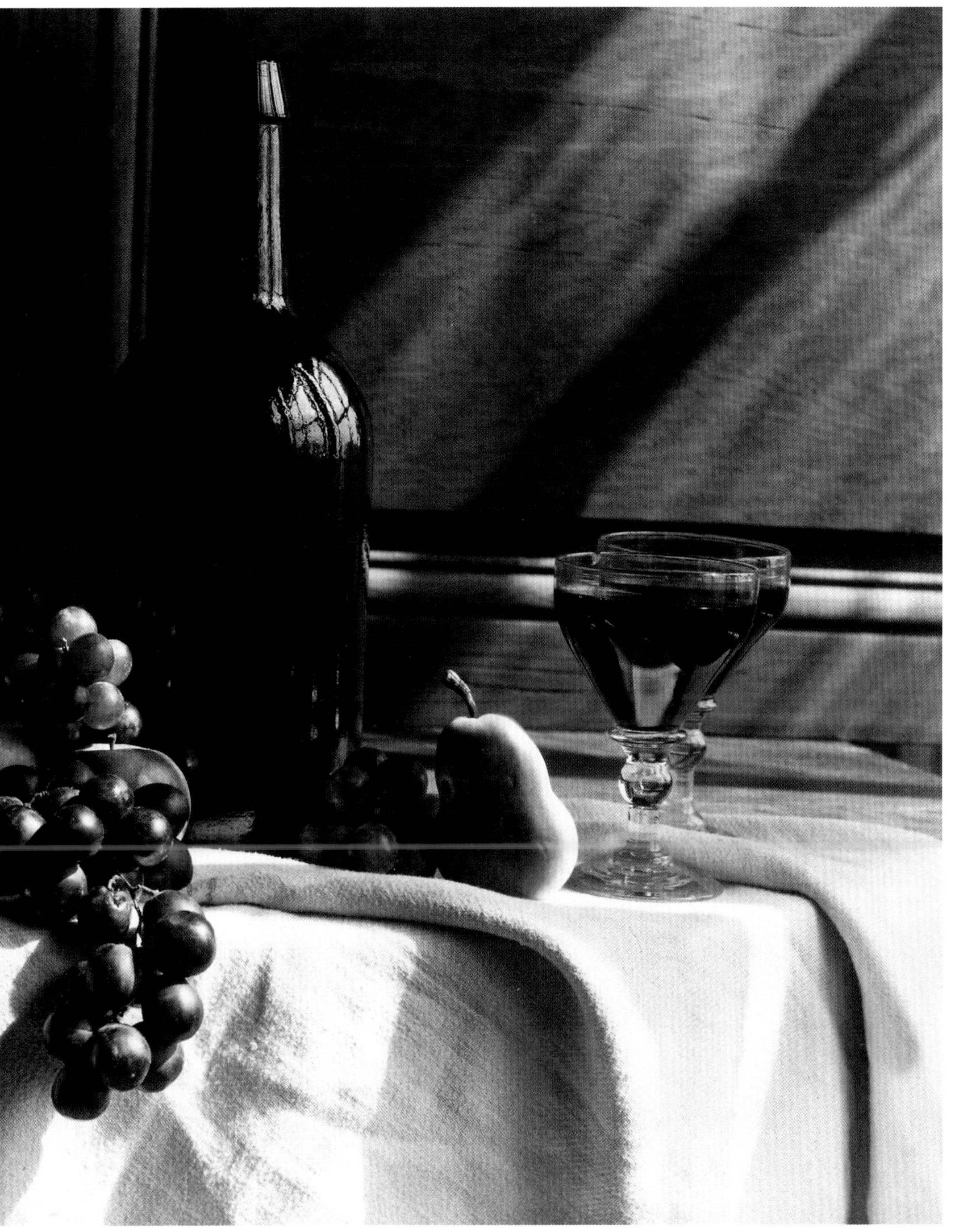

New York Still Life I, 1949

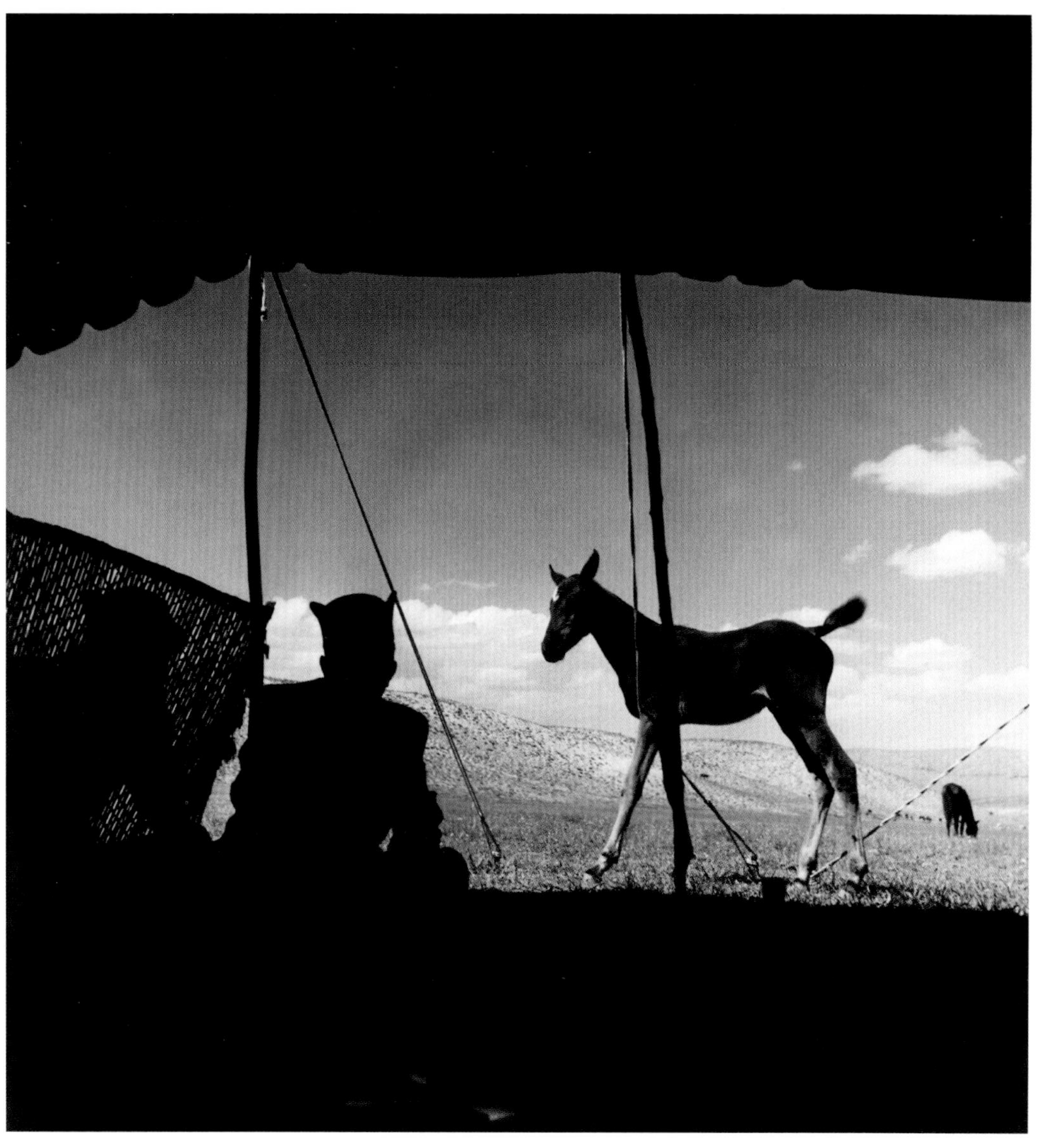

Colt and Qashqa'i tribesmen, 1950

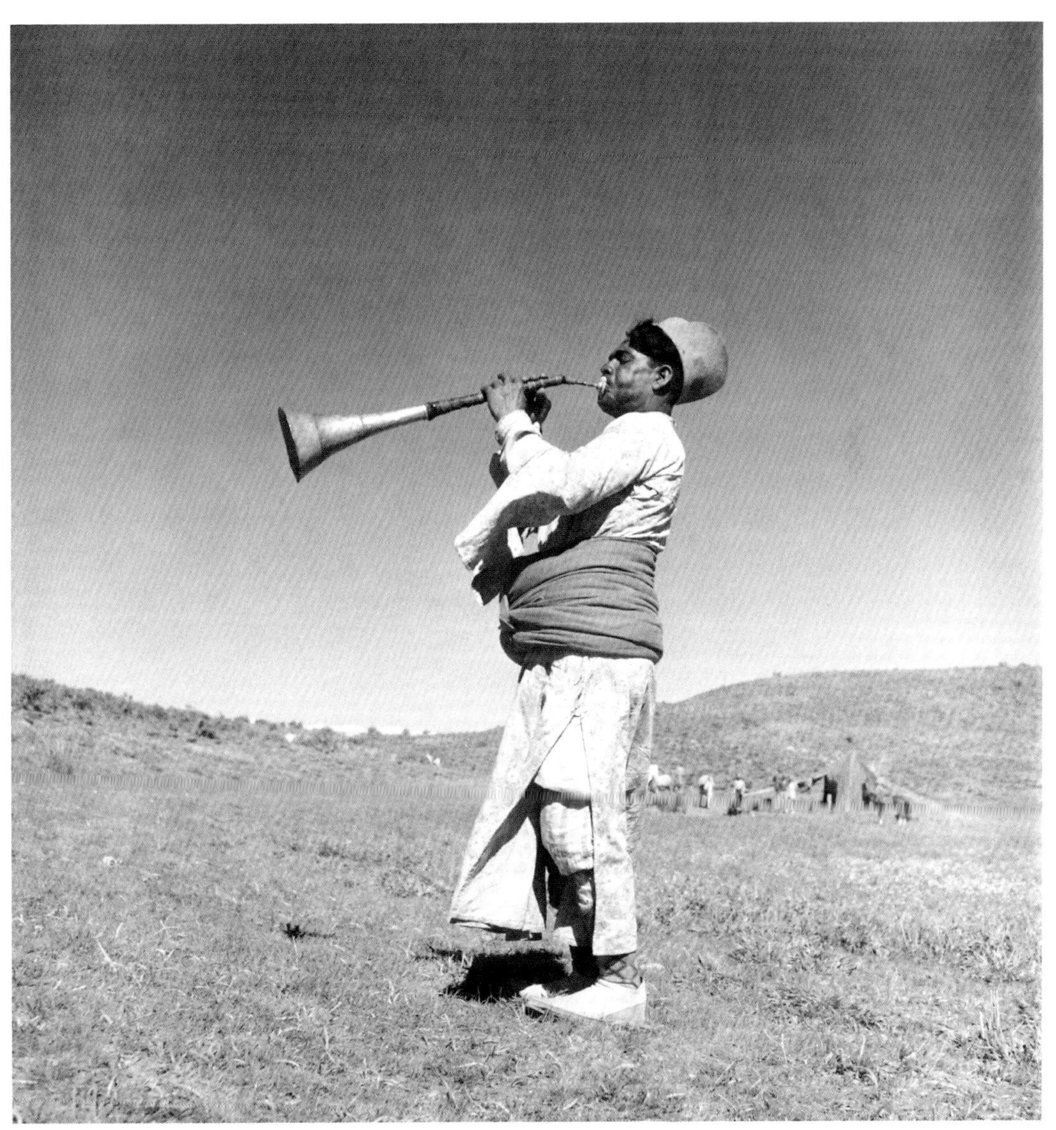

Qashqa'i trumpeter, 1950

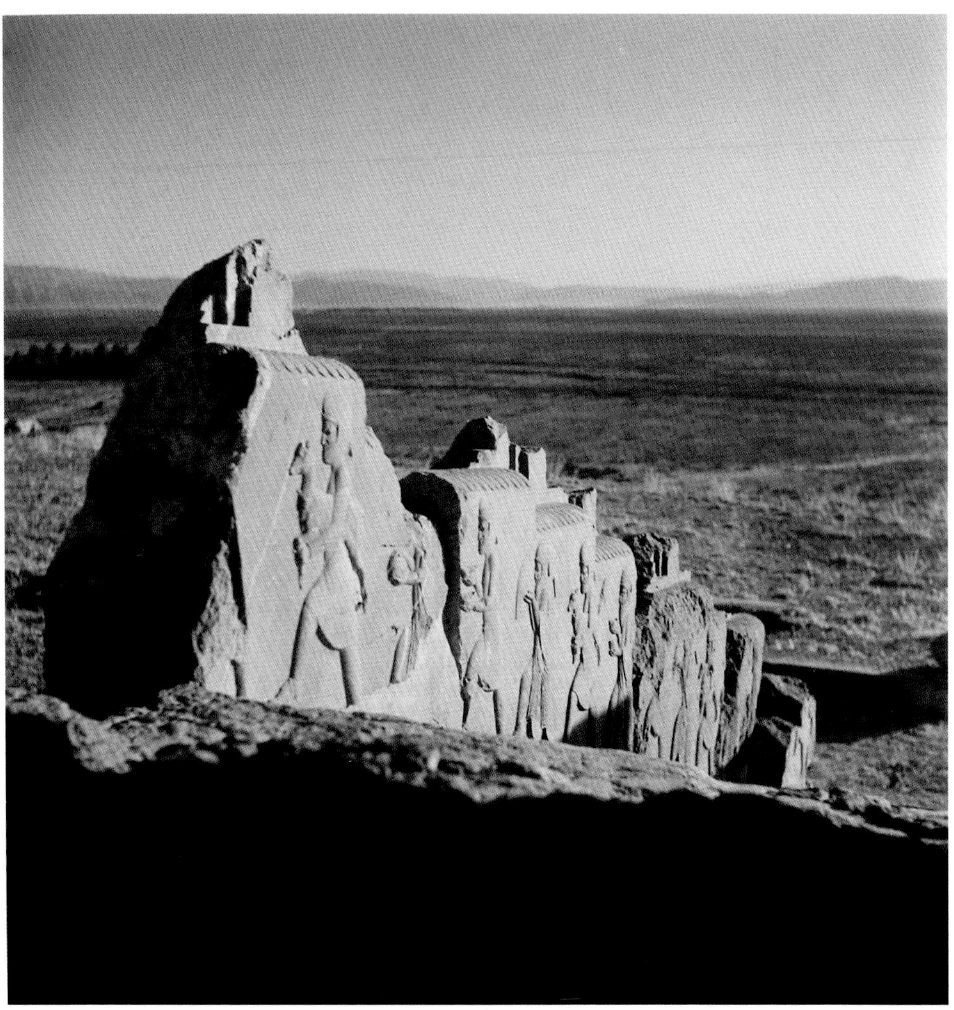

Staircase wall, Persepolis, 1949

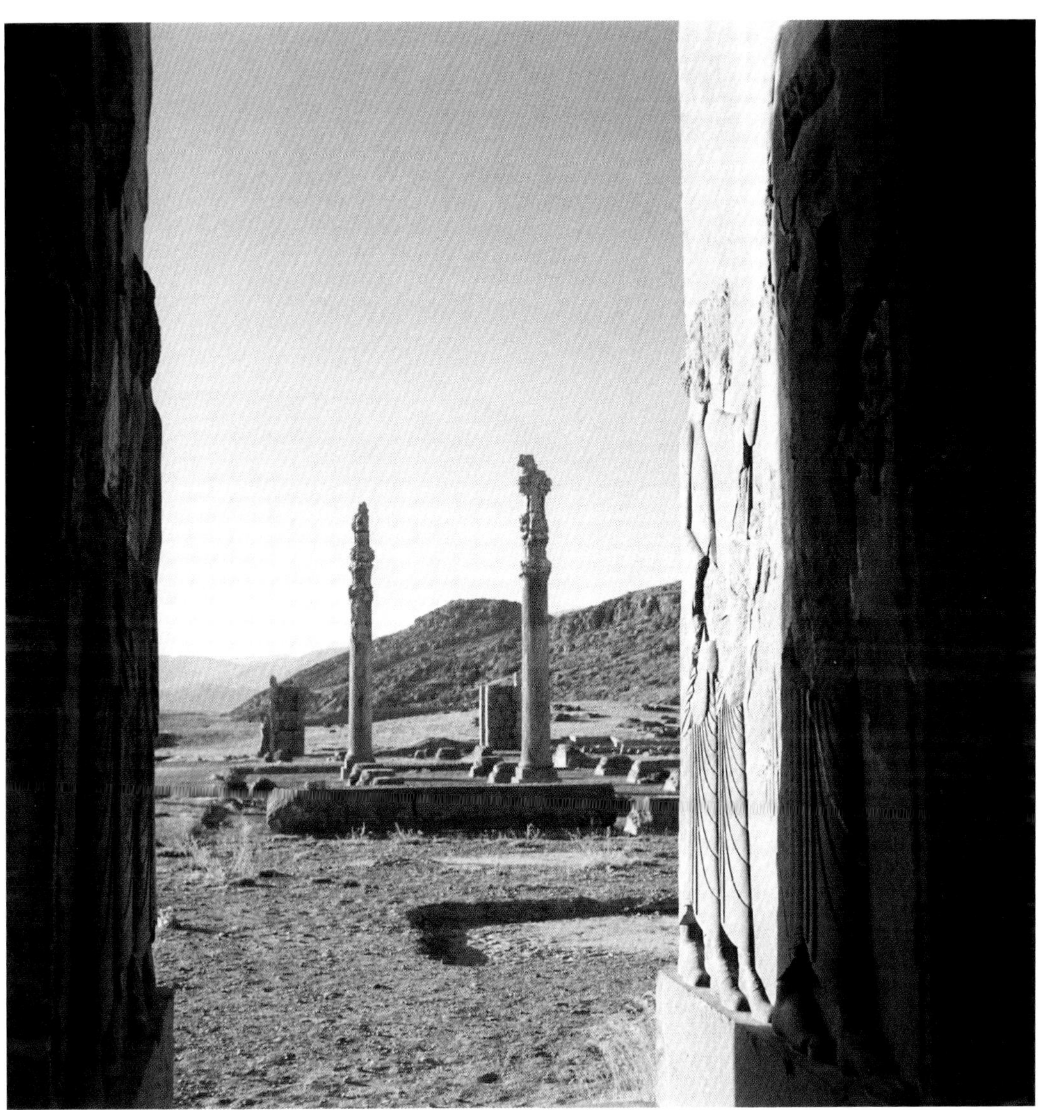

Palace of Persepolis, 1949

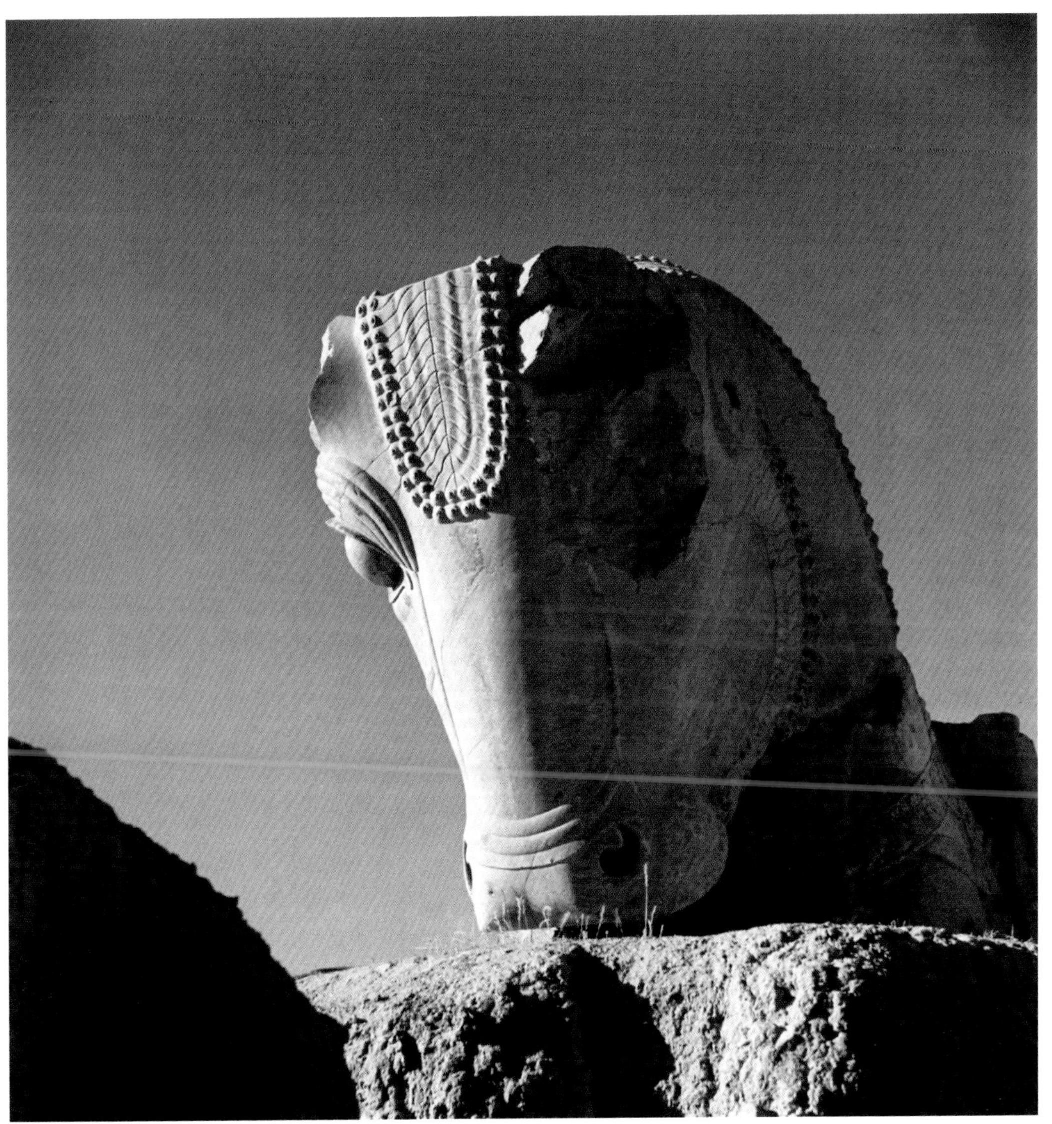

Persepolis Bull, 1949

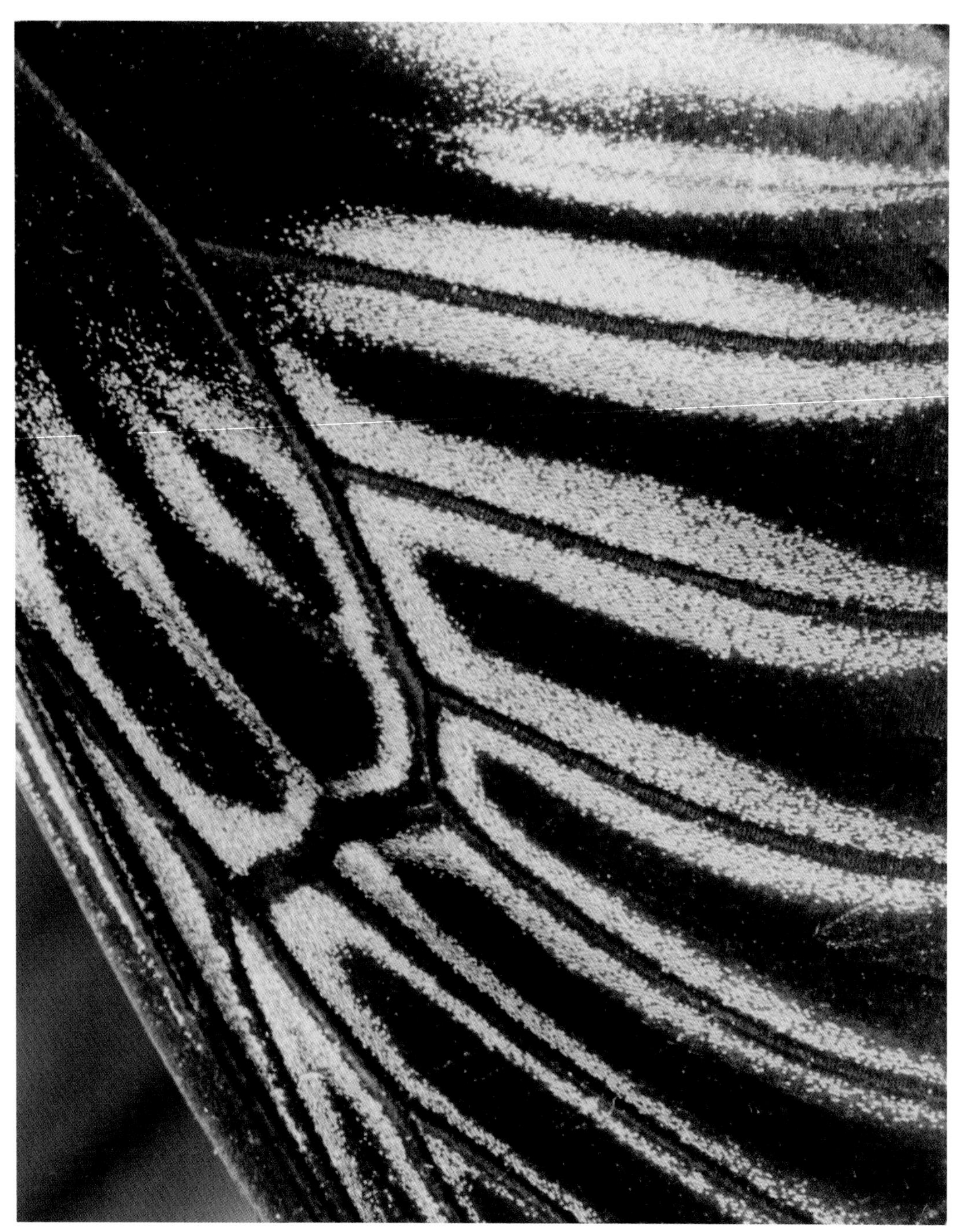

Wing of Ornithoptera Cellularis, Butterfly, 1946

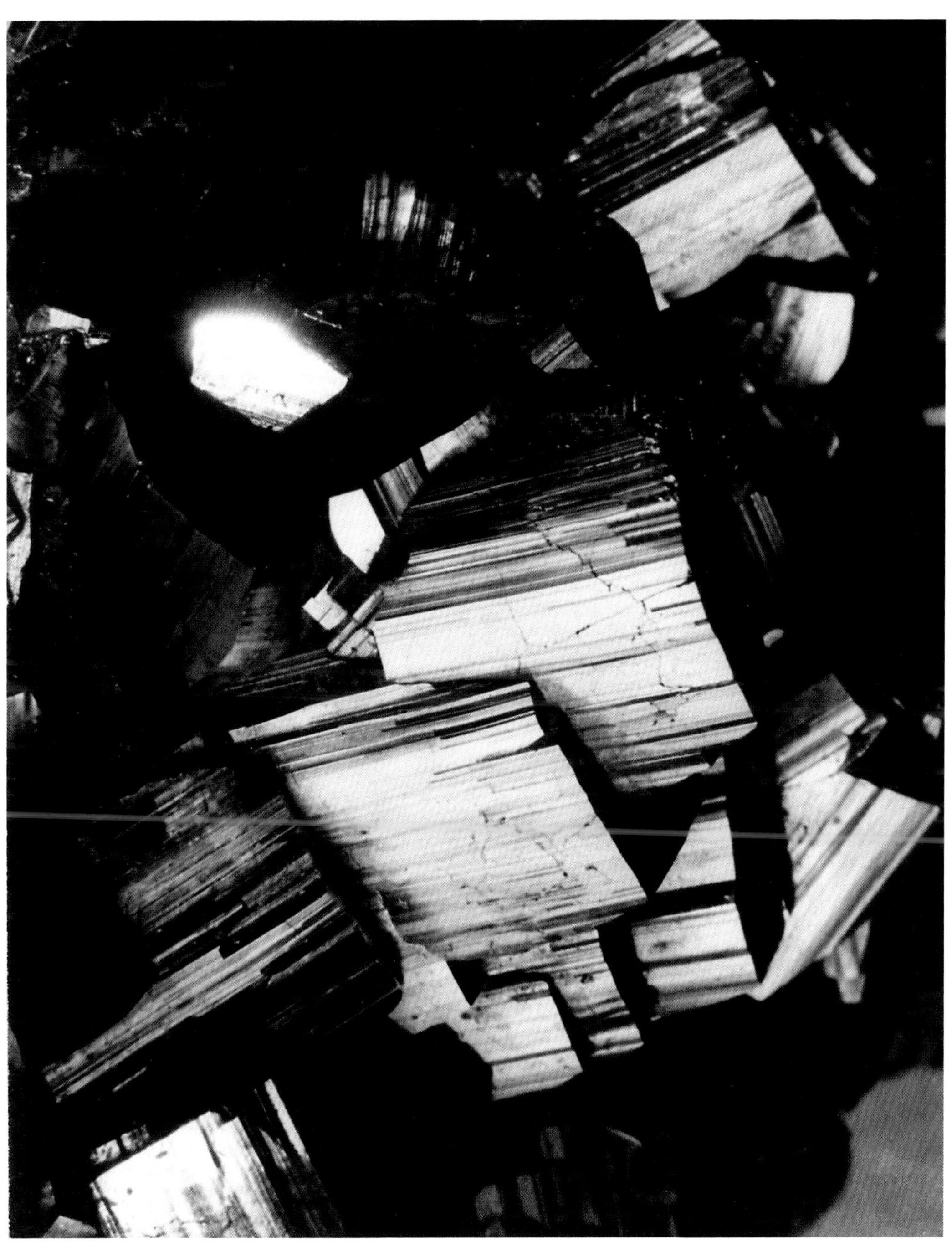

Pyrite, Mineral, 1946

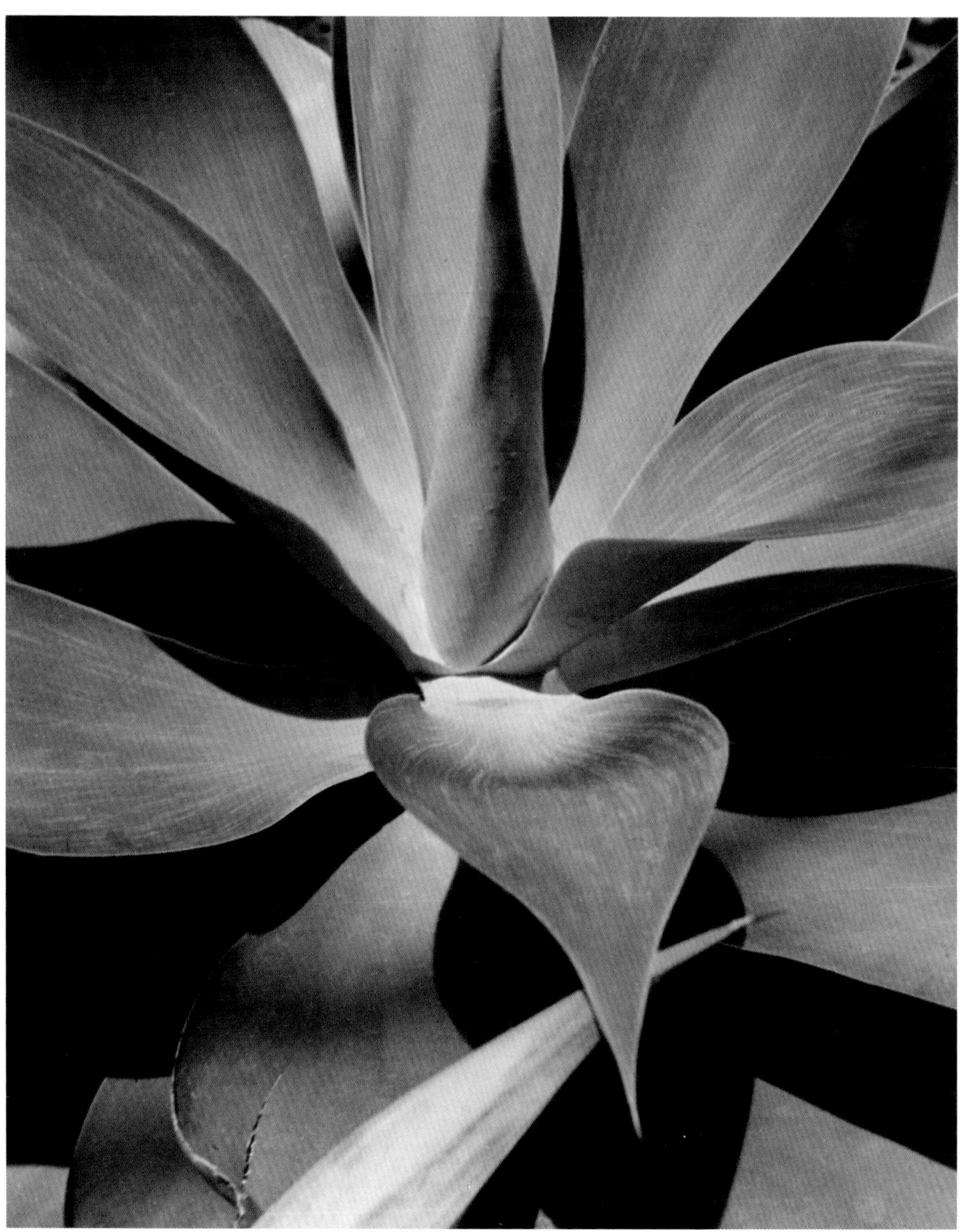

Agave Attenuata, 1946

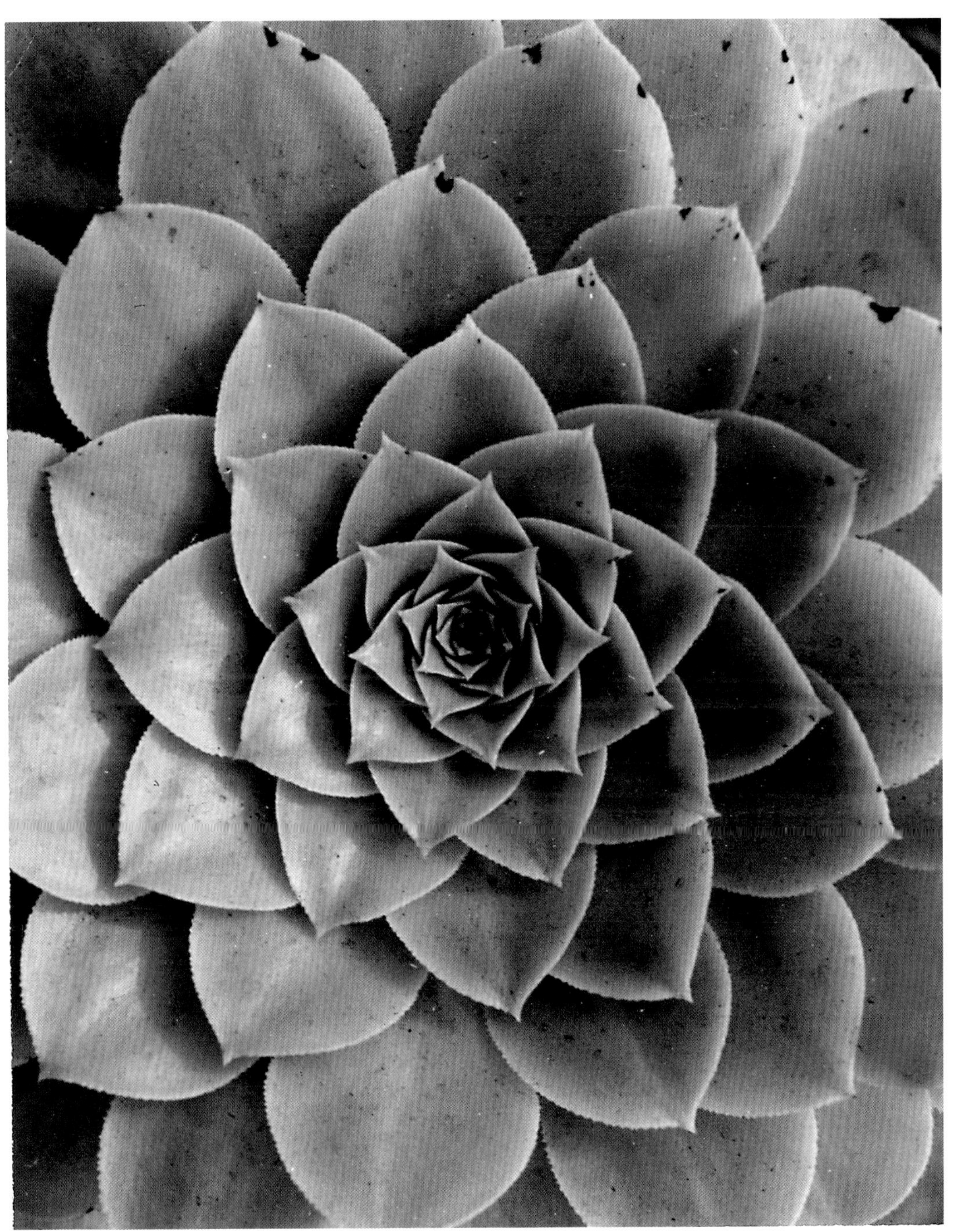

Trichocereus Candicans, 1946

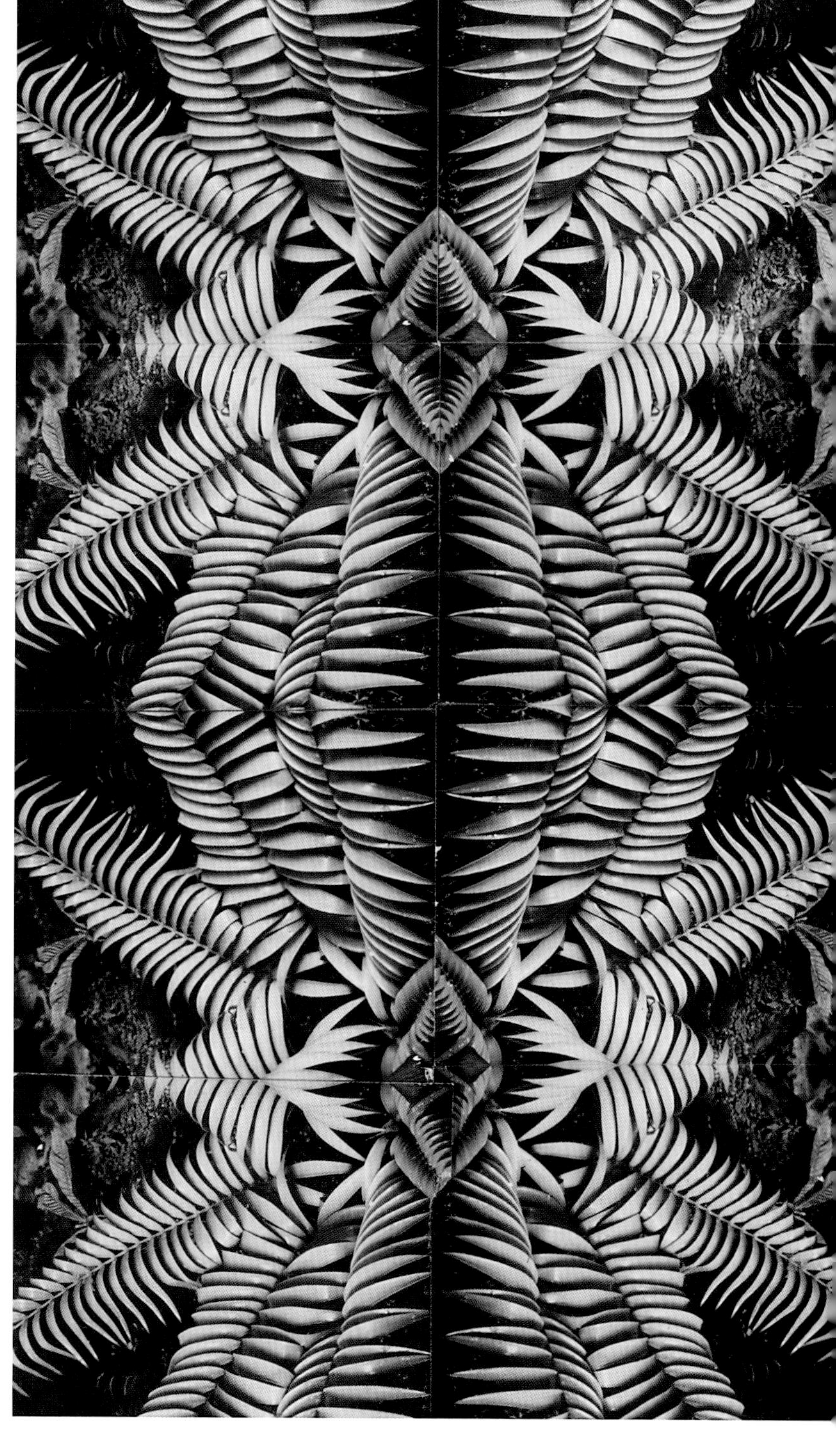

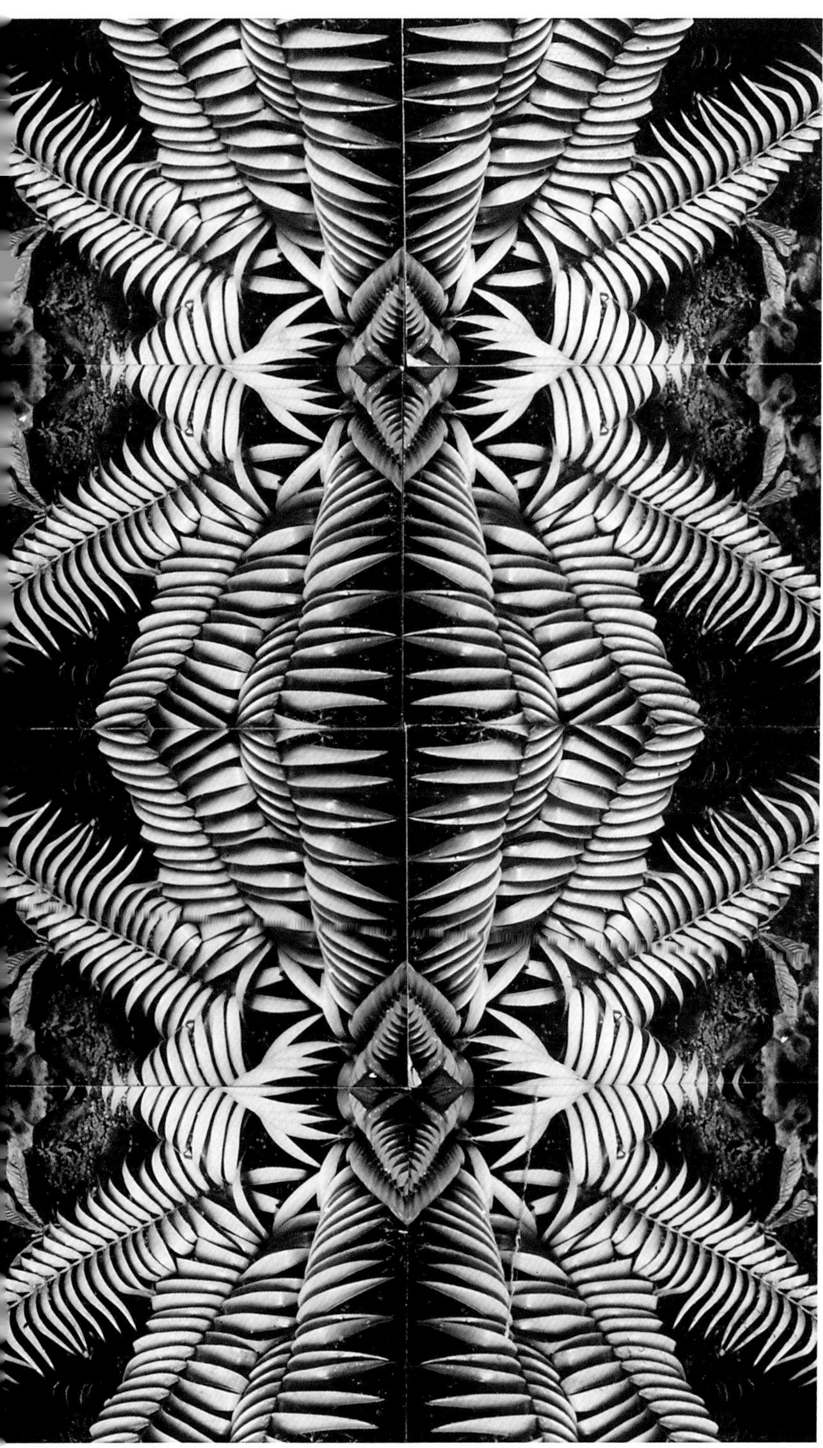

Photographic Pattern, 1946

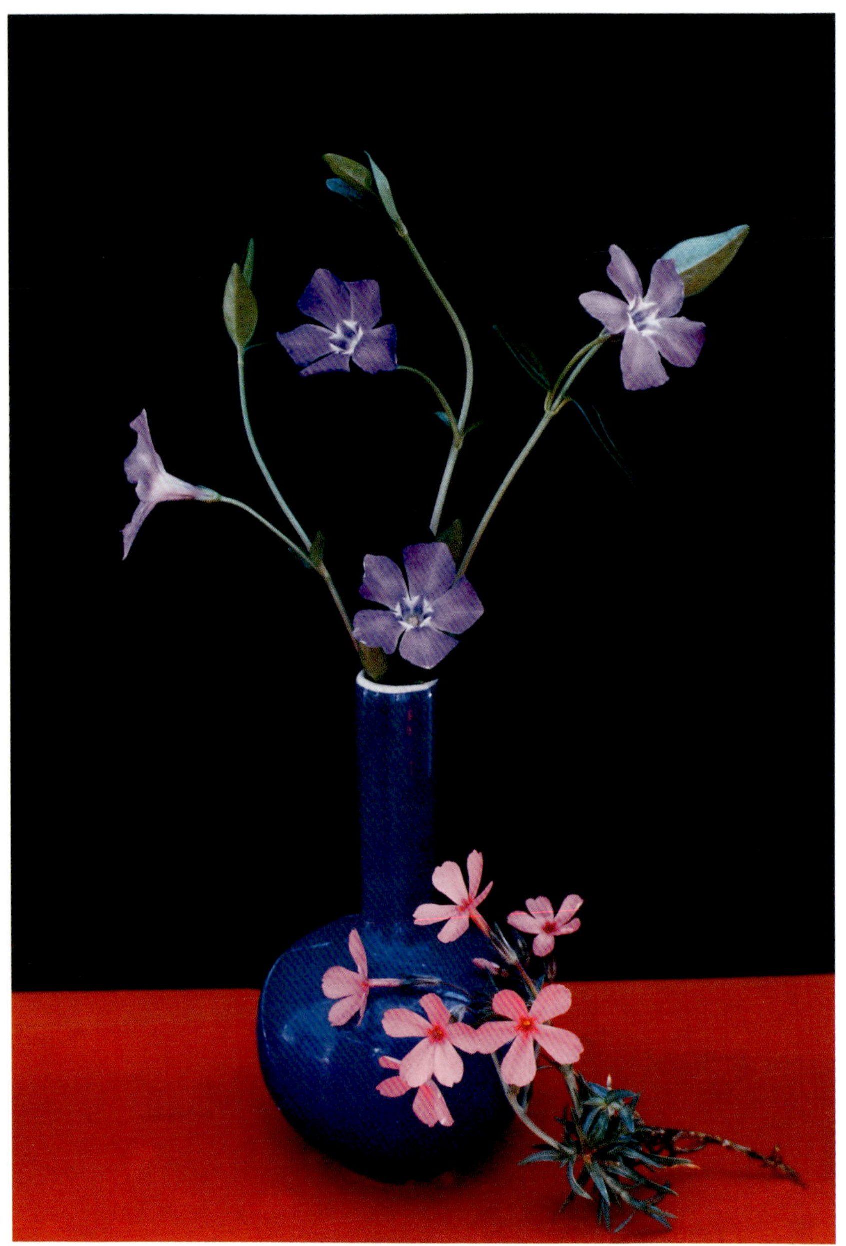

Still Life, 1980s

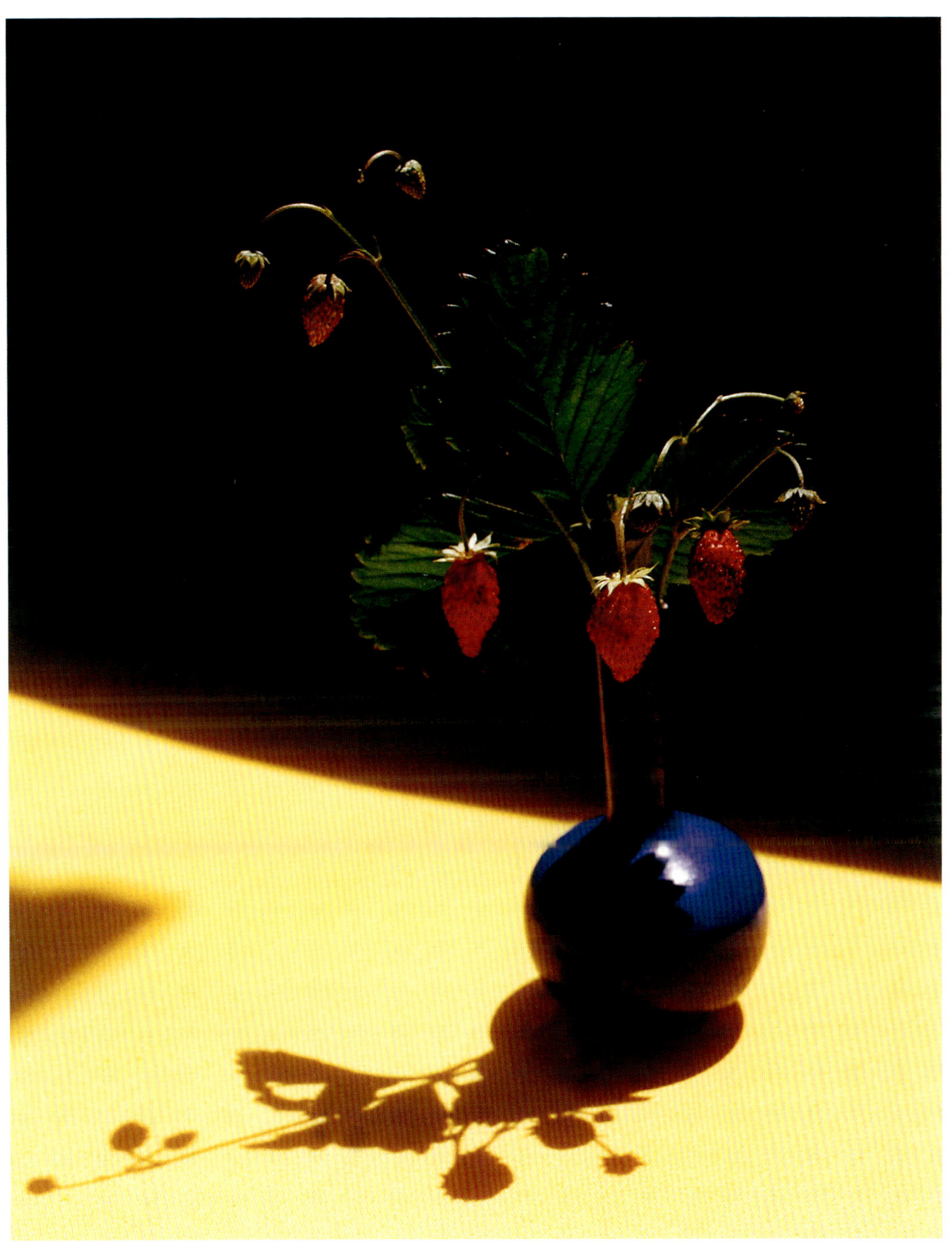

Still Life, 1980s

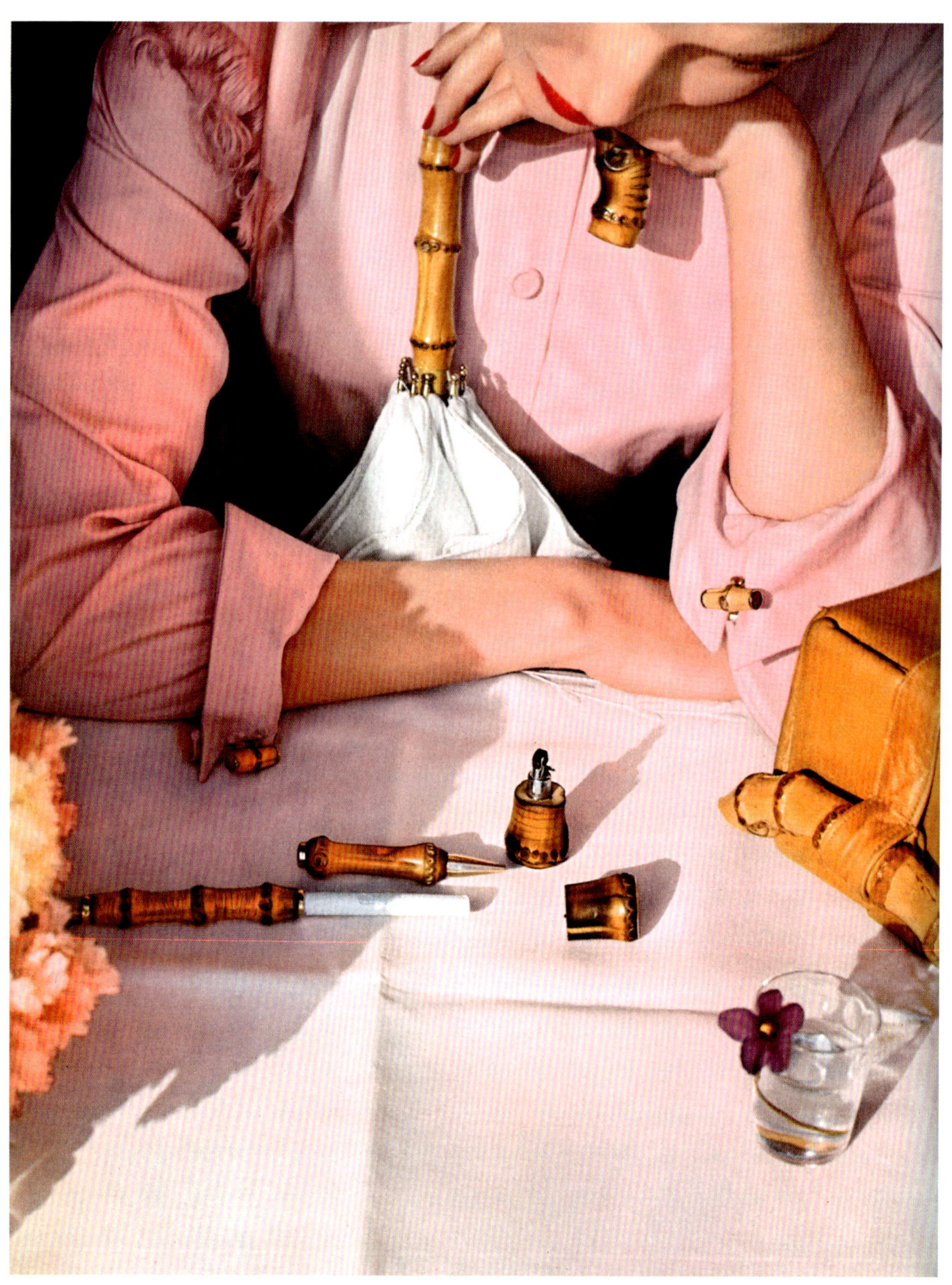

Bamboo accessories by Cartier, 1949

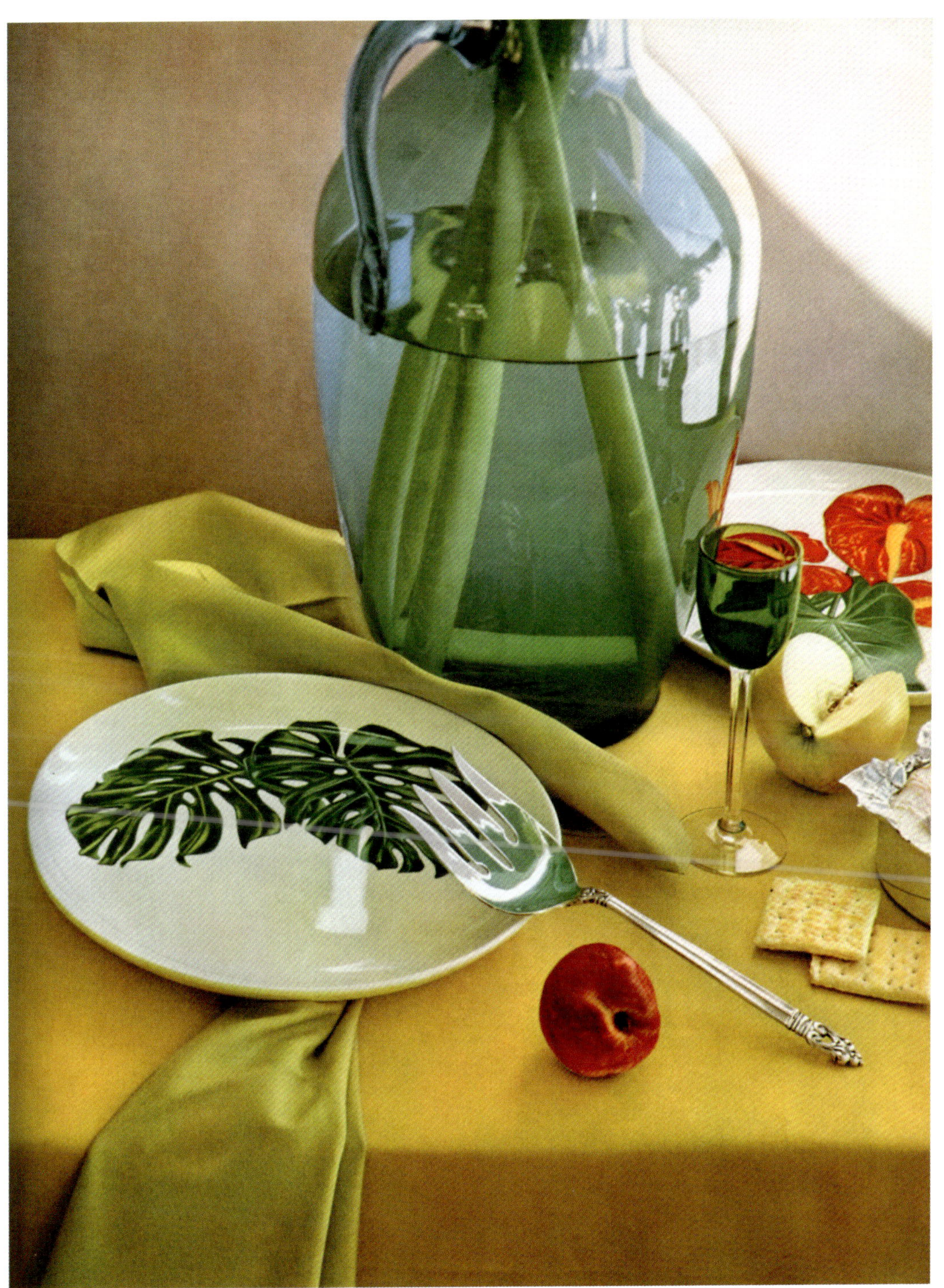

Still Life, *c.* 1950

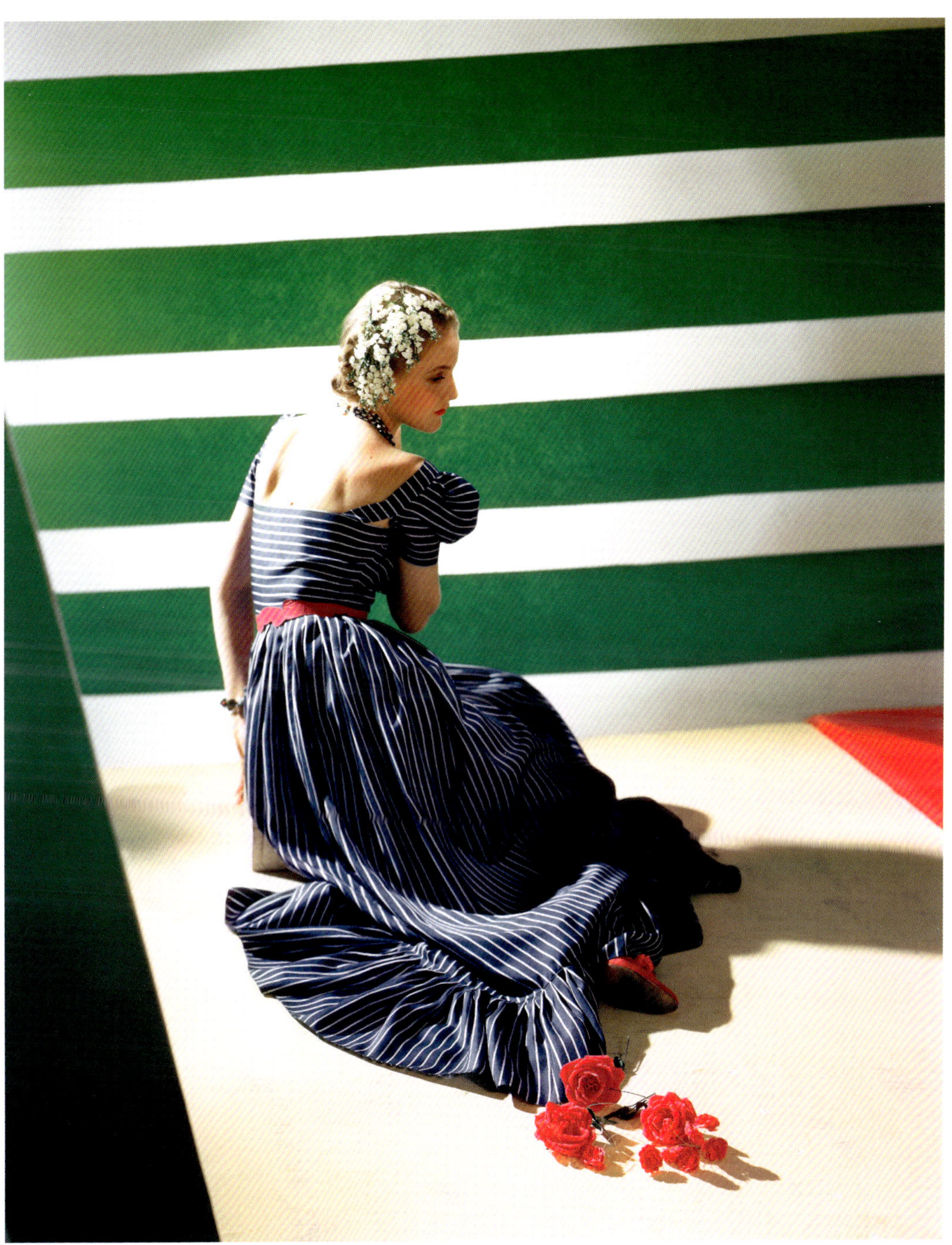

Dress by Hattie Carnegie, 1939

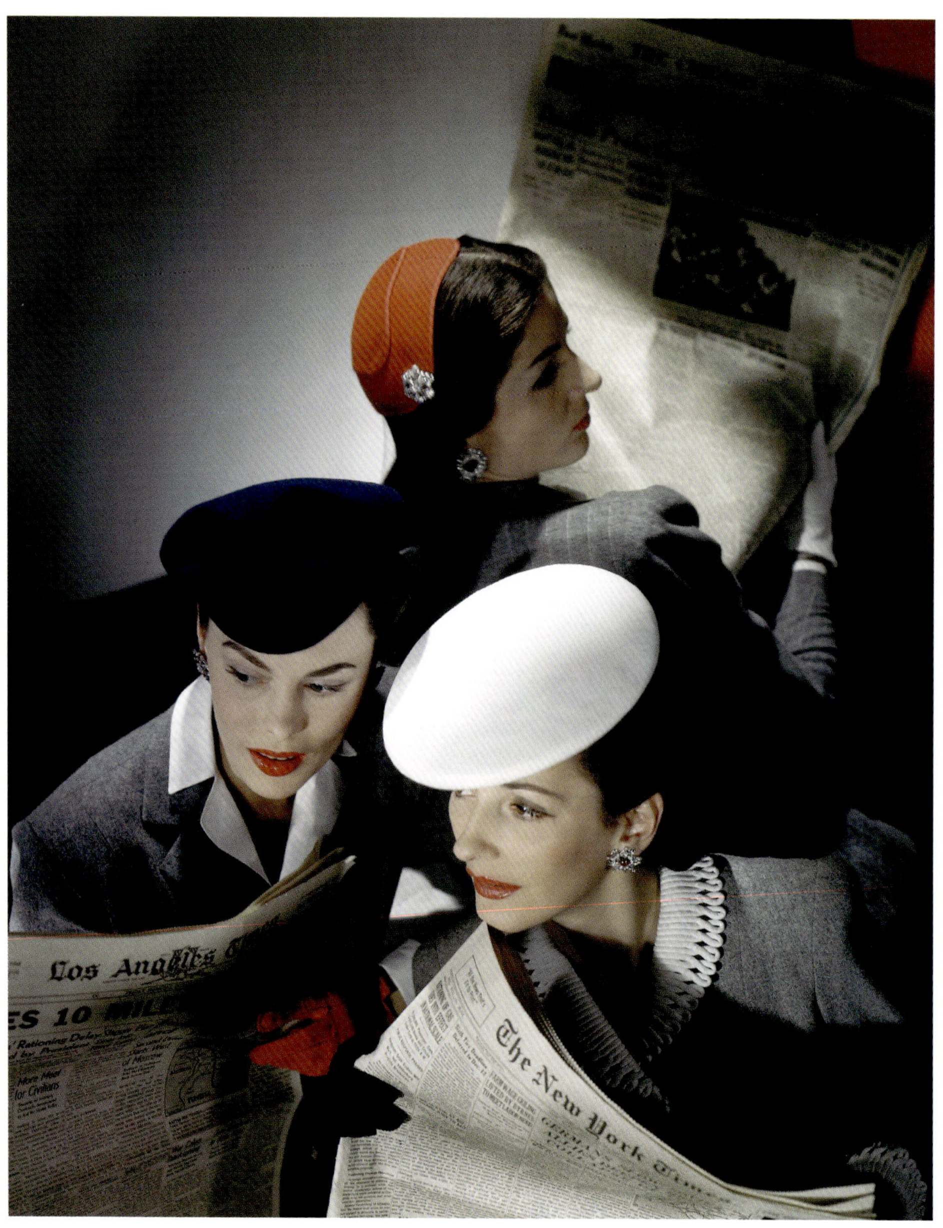

Hats by Best, Lord and Taylor and Mme. Pauline, gloves by Dawnelle, 1943

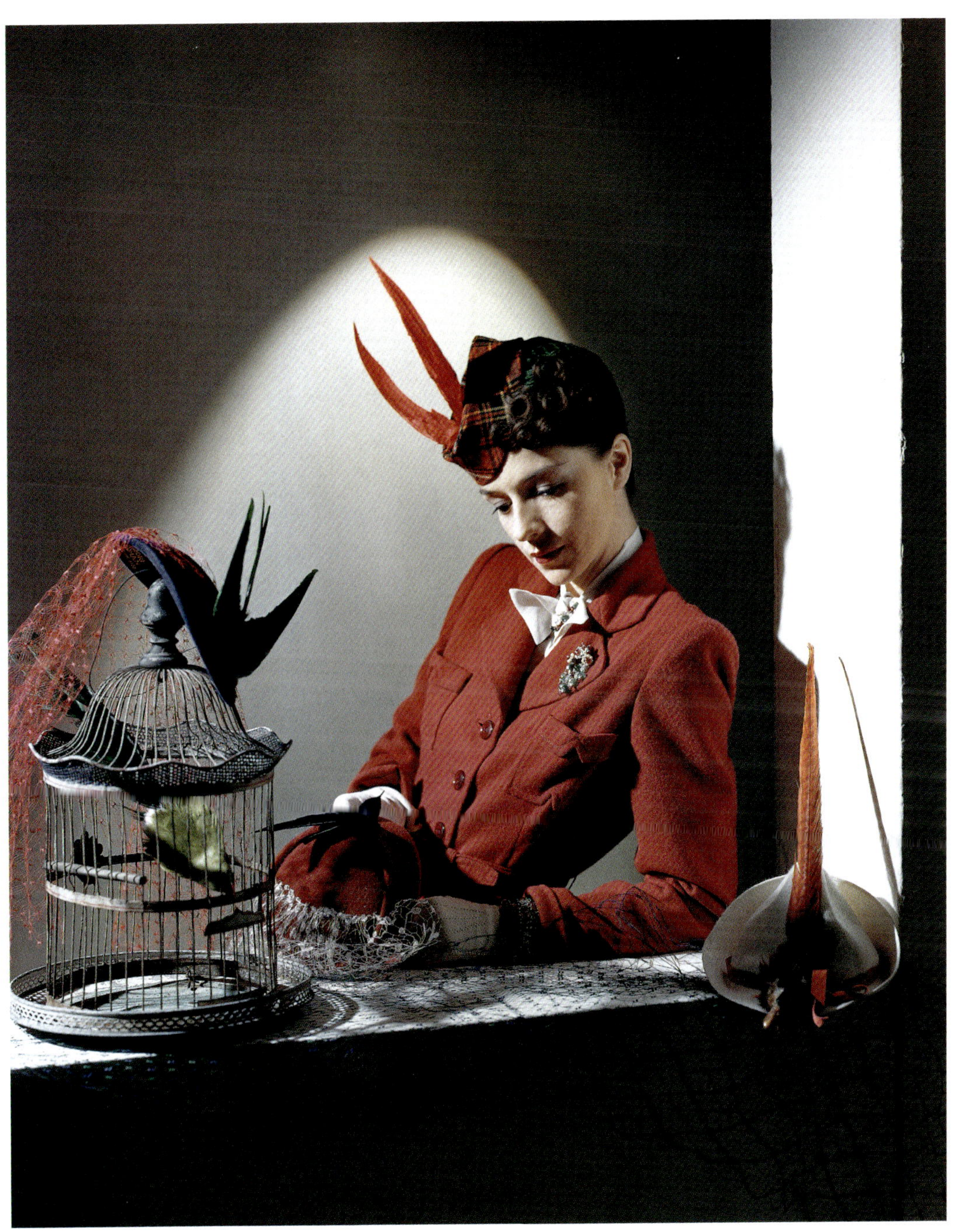

Ensemble by Bergdorf Goodman, jewellery by Cartier, 1939

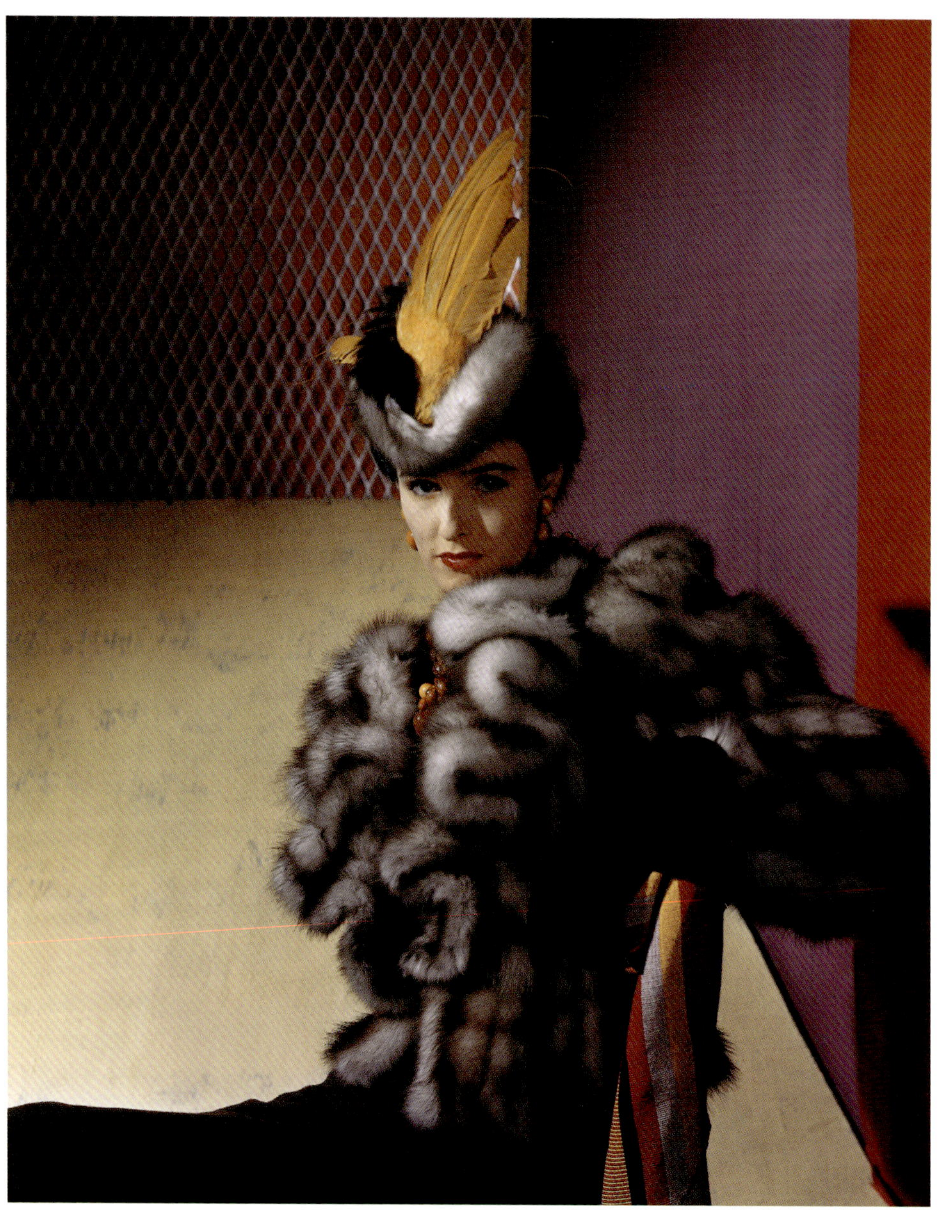

Babe Paley, jacket by Gunther, hat by John Frederics, jewelley by Olga Tritt, 1939

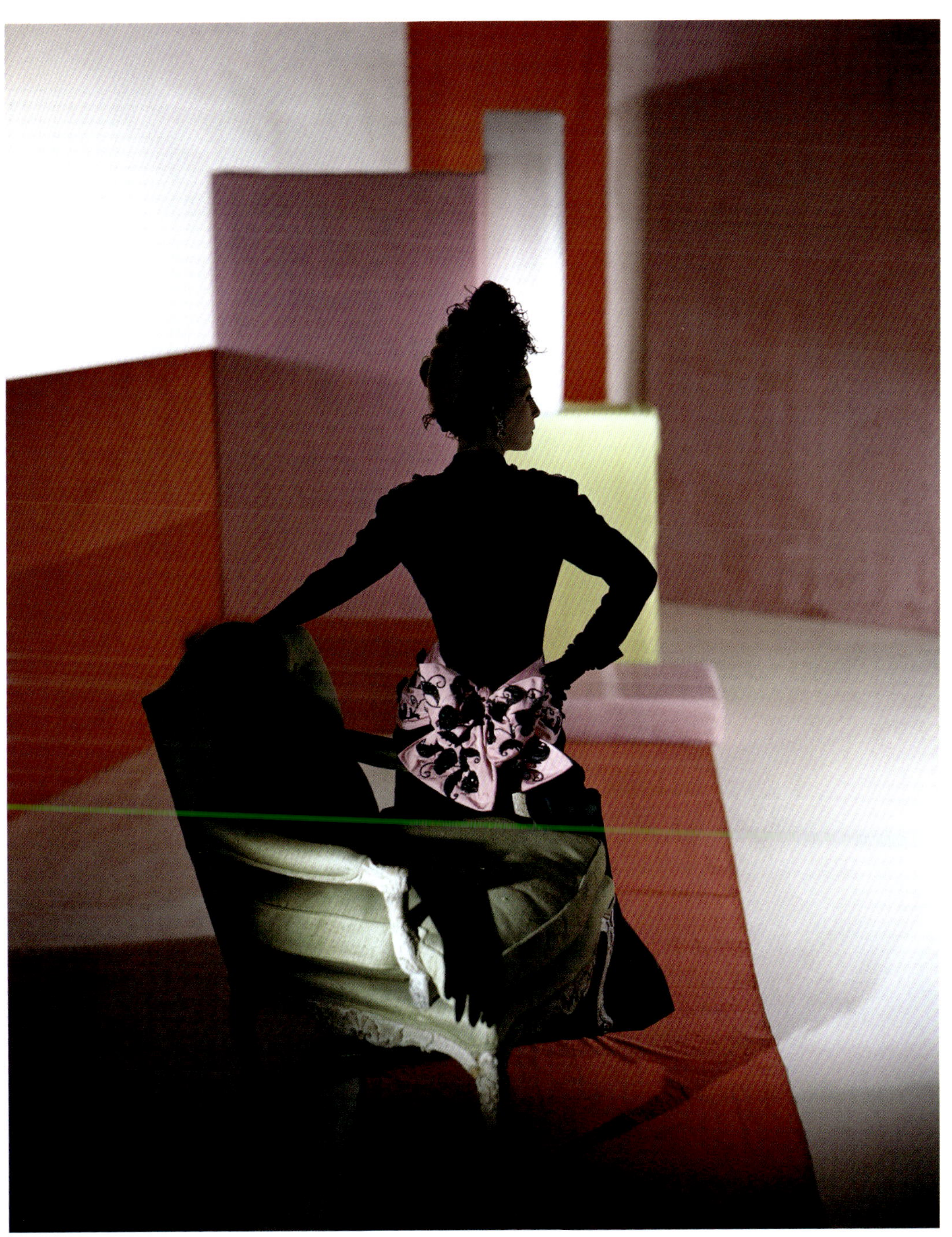

Dinner suit and headdress by Schiaparelli, 1947

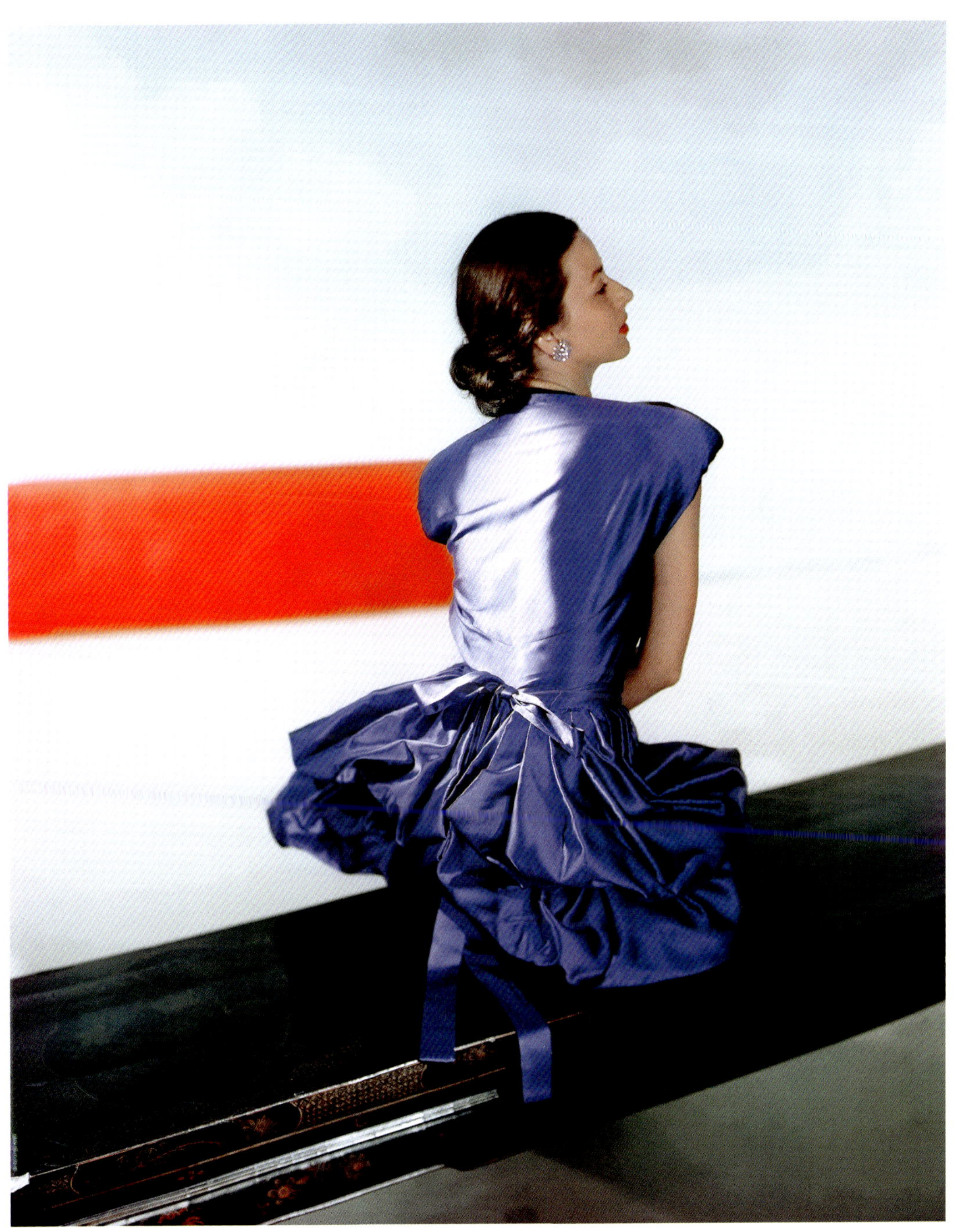

Dorian Leigh, dress by Henri Bendel, 1946

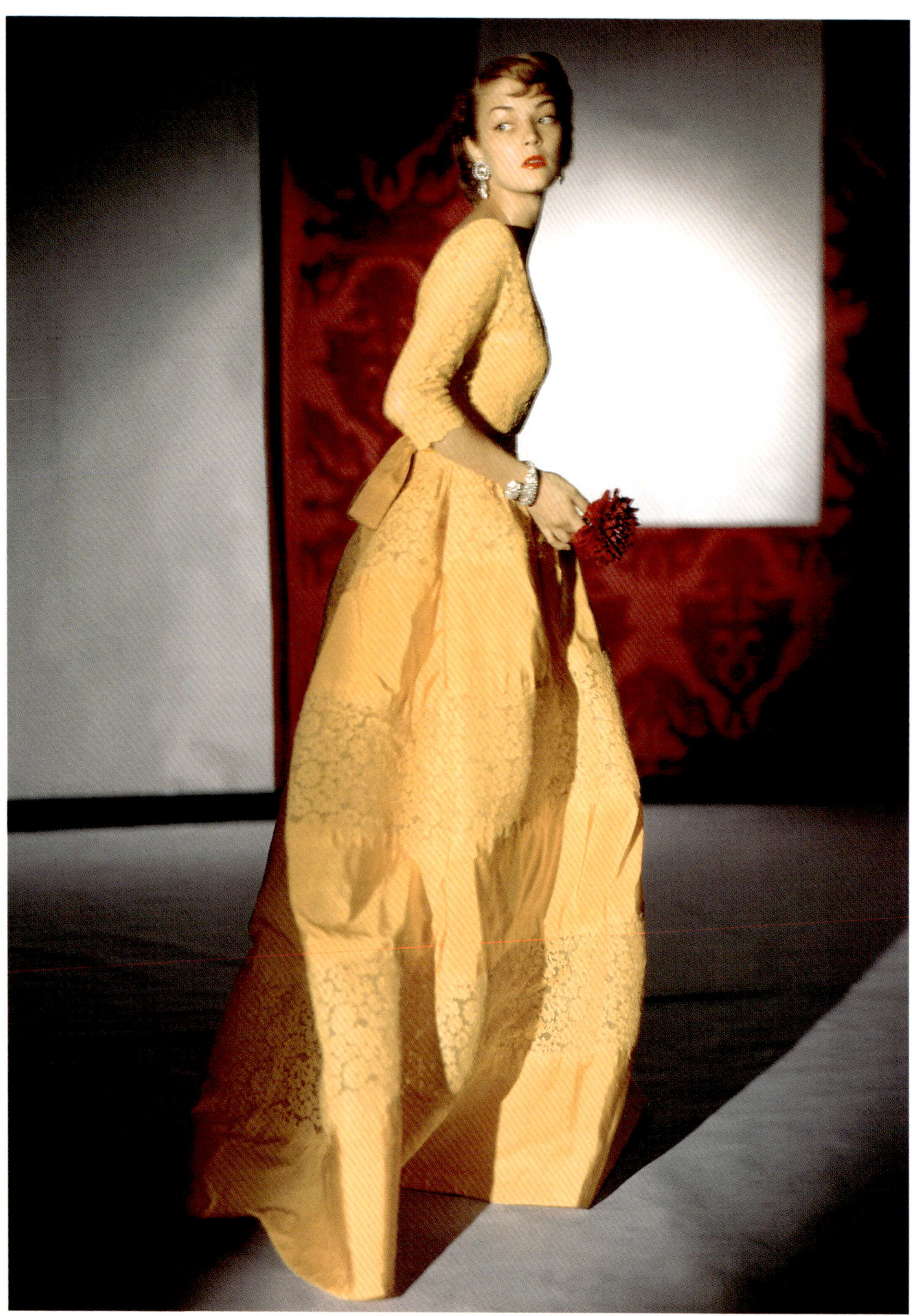

Dress by Henri Bendel, jewellery by Harry Winston, 1948

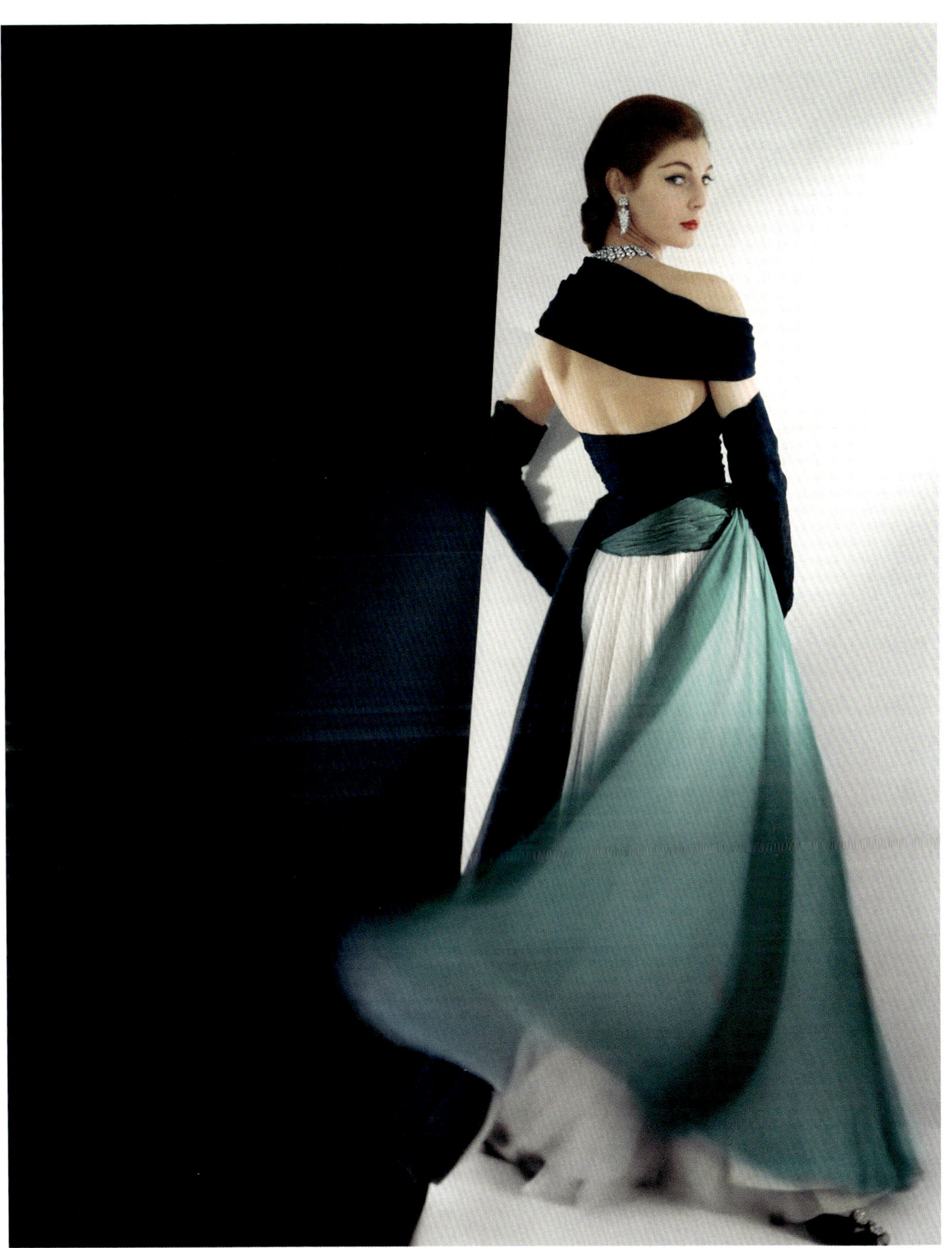

Dress by Jean Dessès, 1952

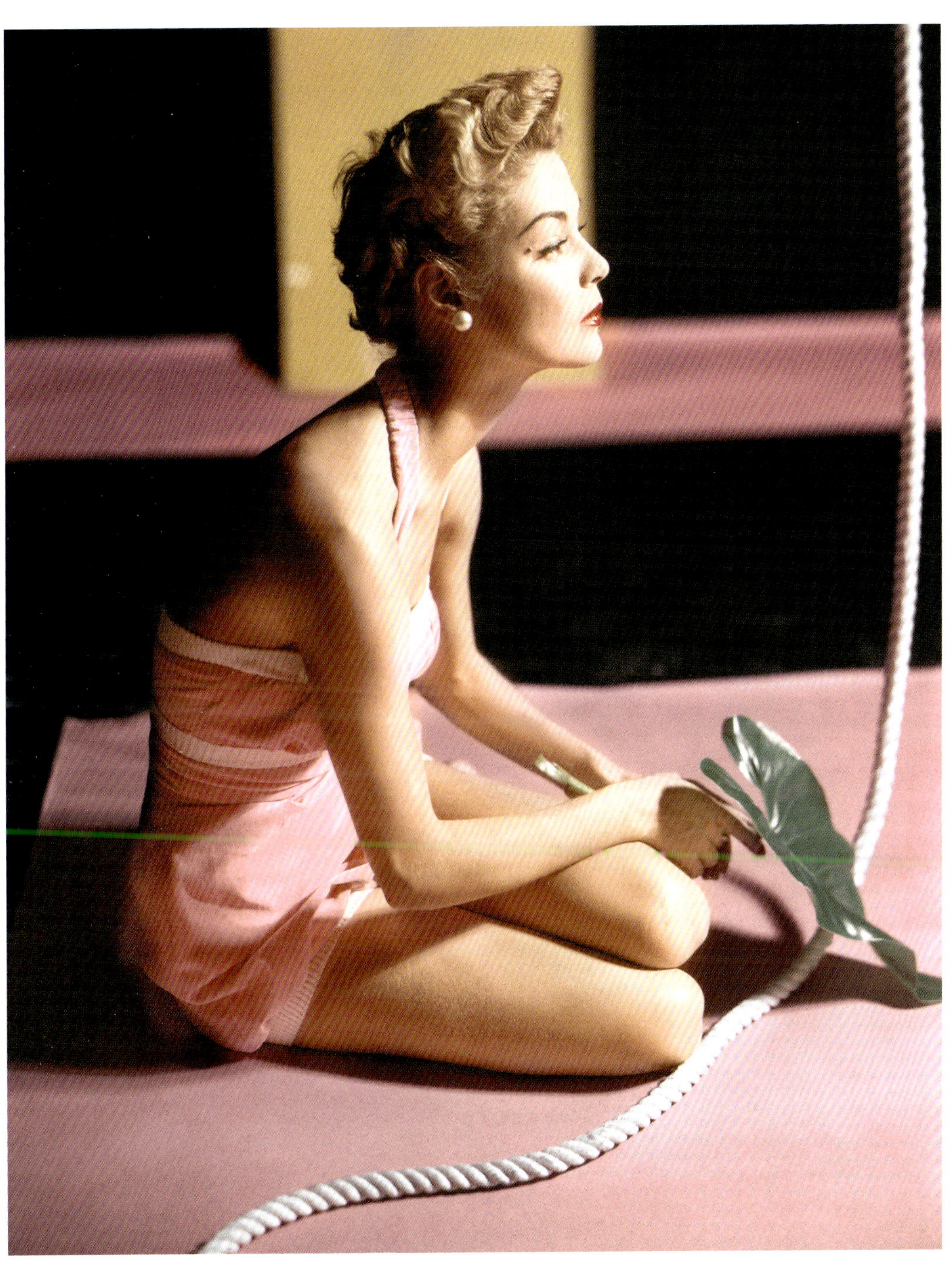

Jean Patchett, bathing suit by Brigance, 1951

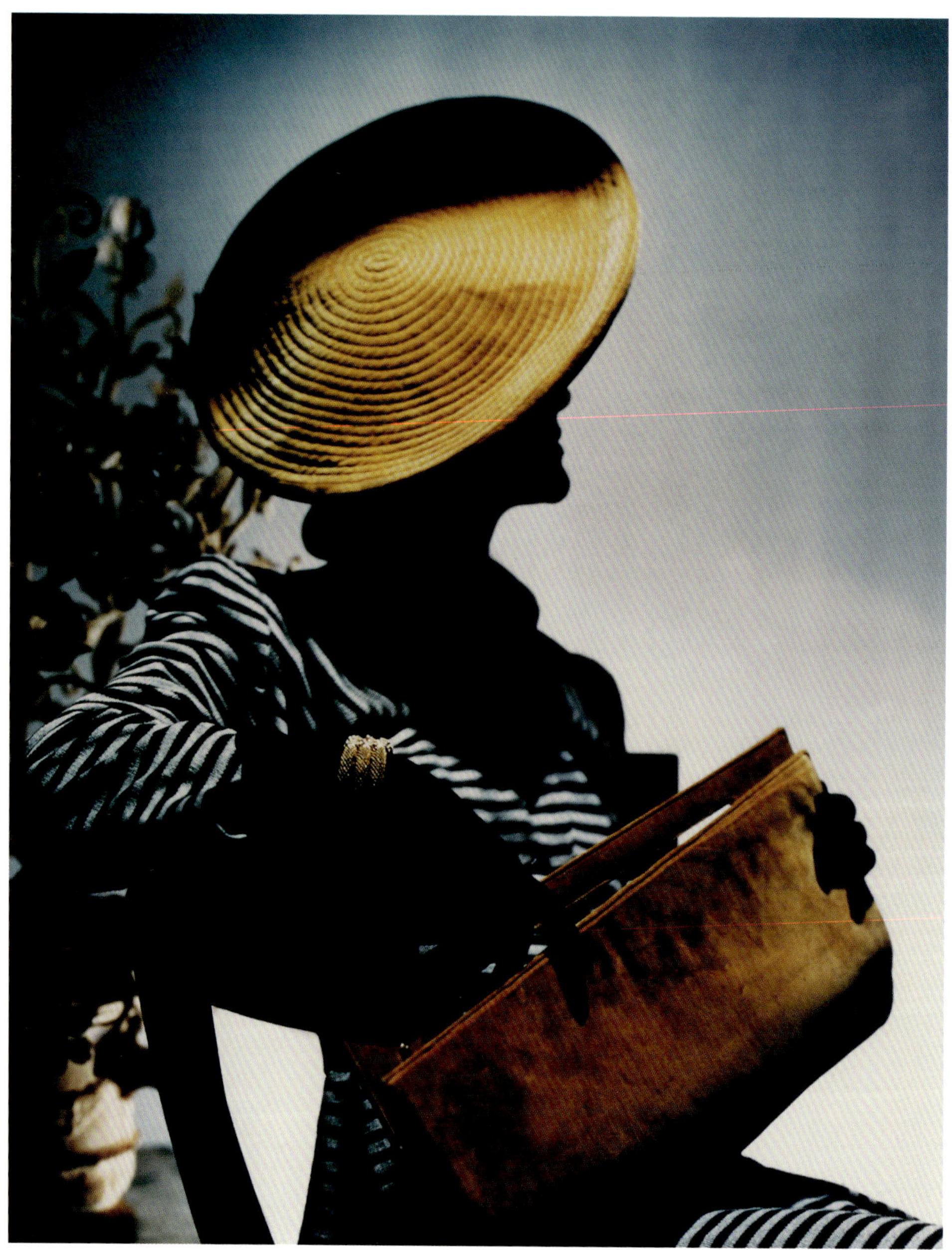

Fashion, 1940s

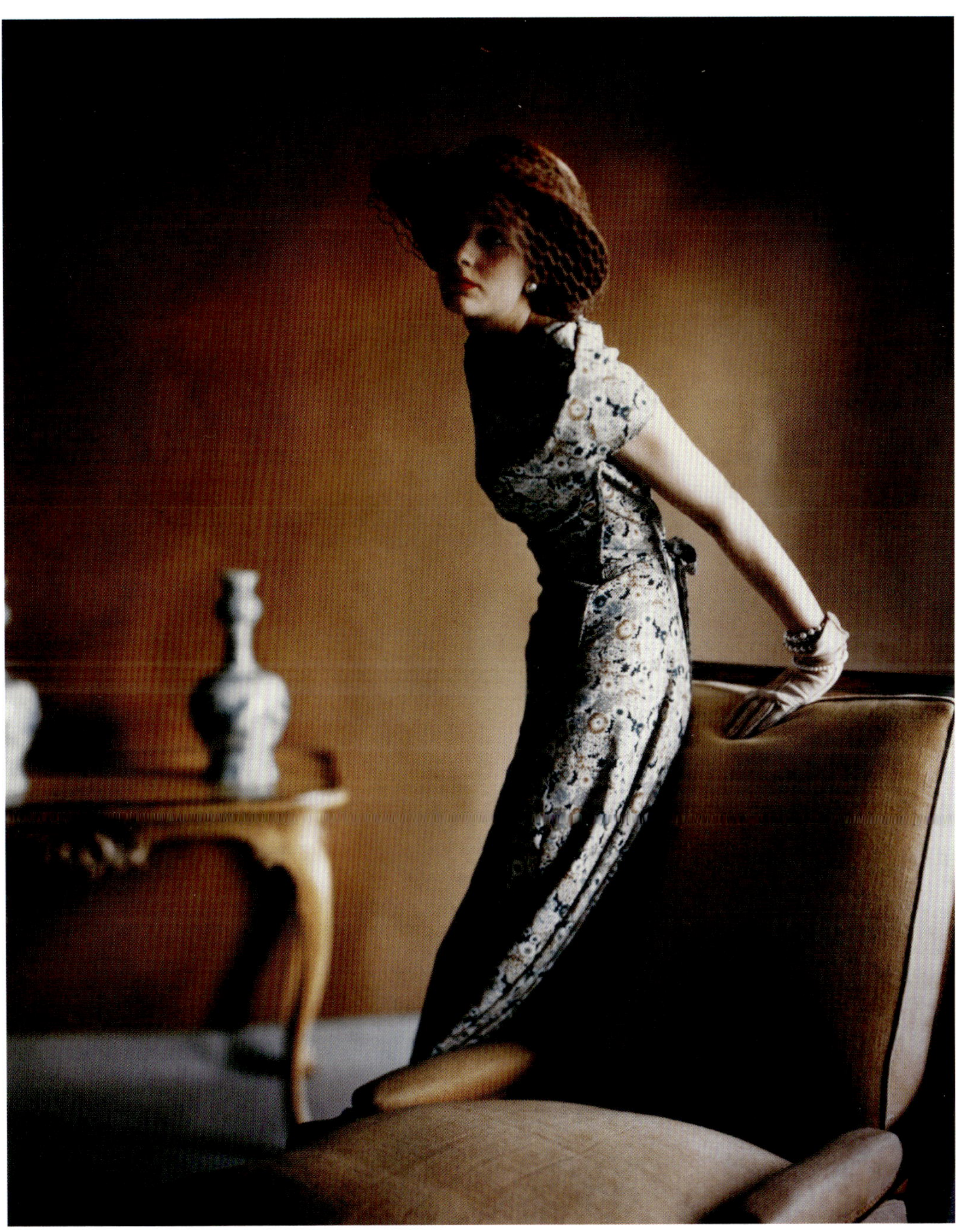

Dress by B.H. Wragge, hat by Sally Victor, gloves by Wear-Right, 1948

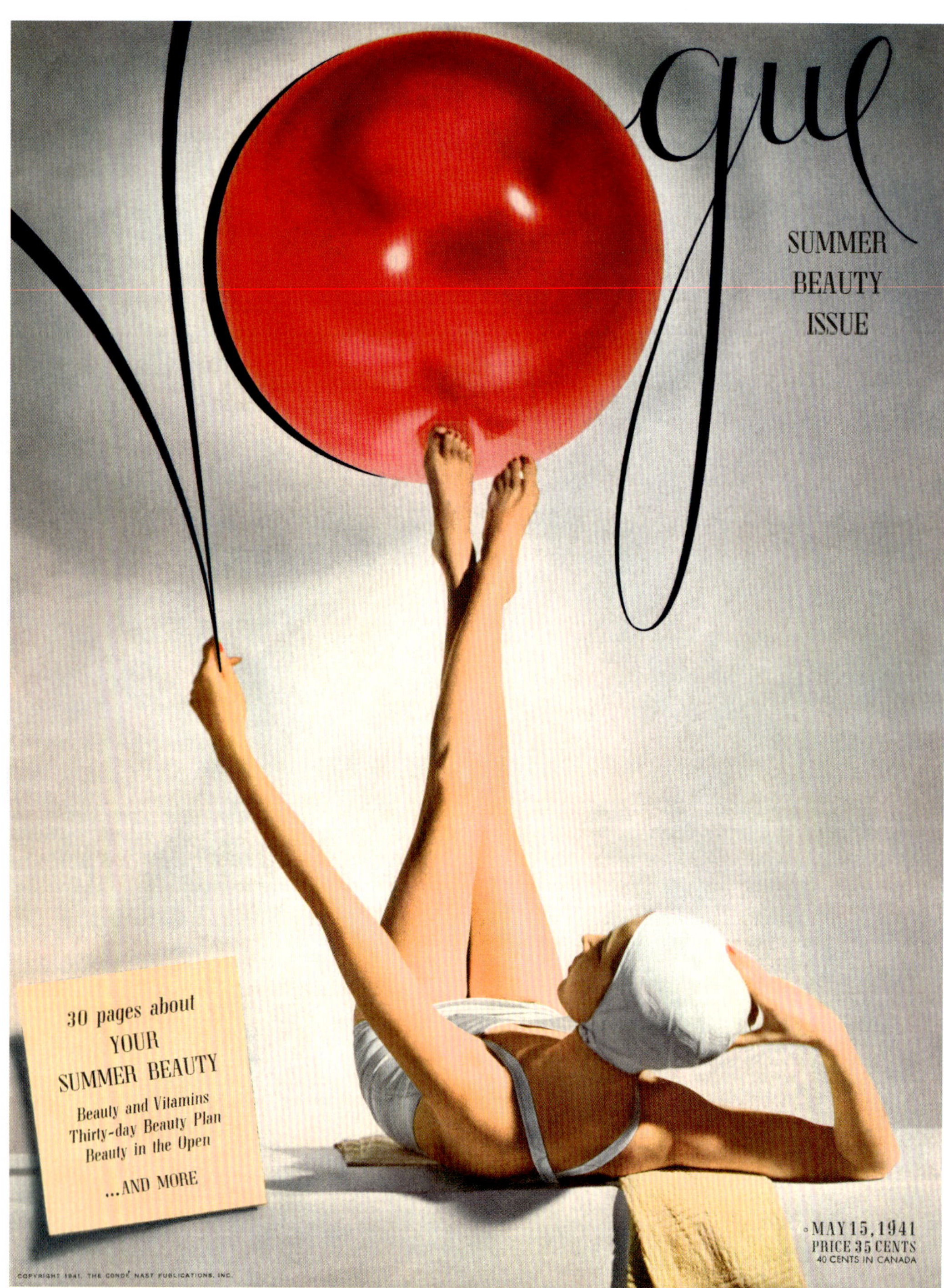

American *Vogue* cover, 15 May 1941

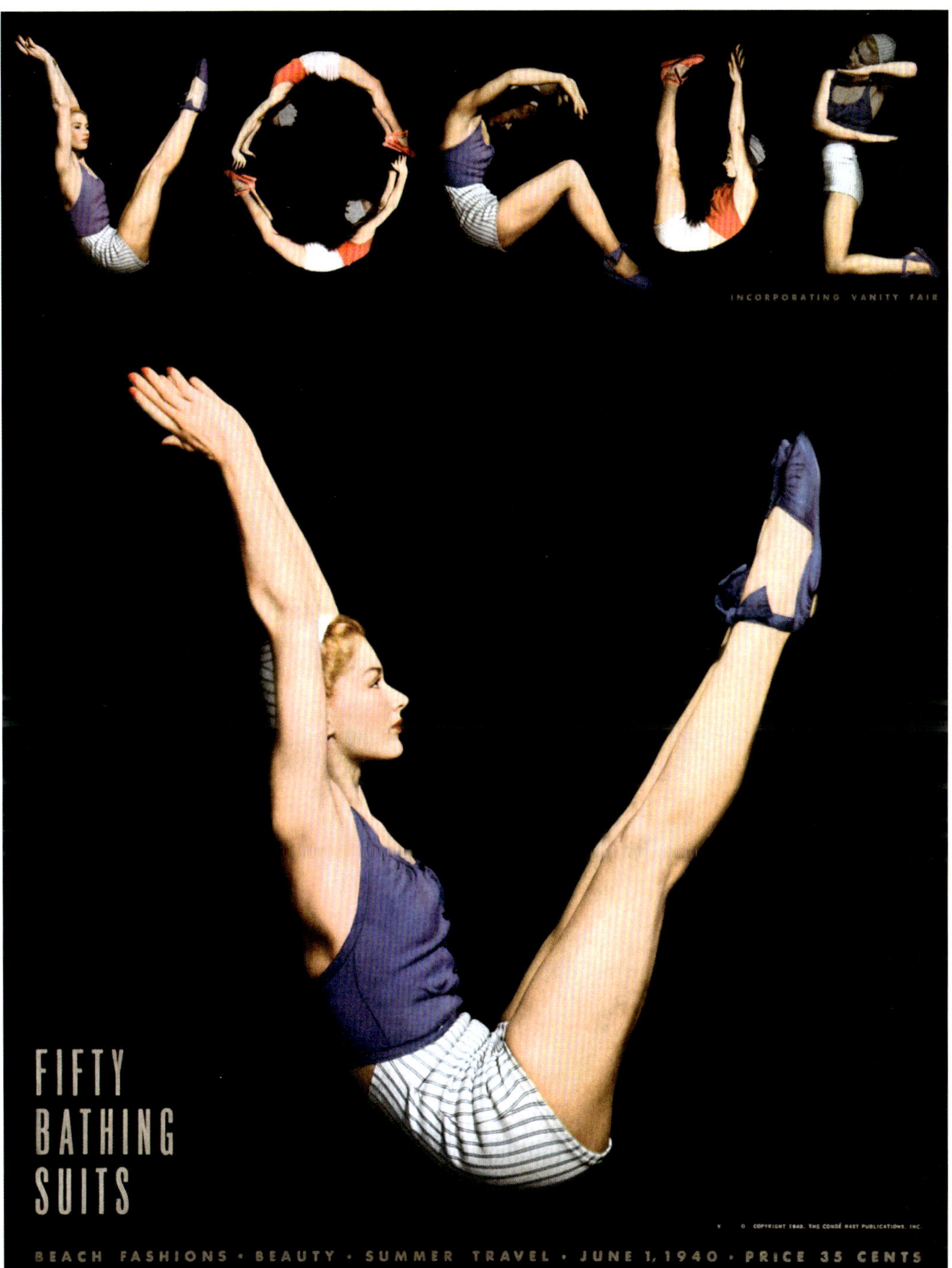

American *Vogue* cover, 1 June 1940
Lisa Fonssagrives, bathing suit by Brigance, shoes by Joyce

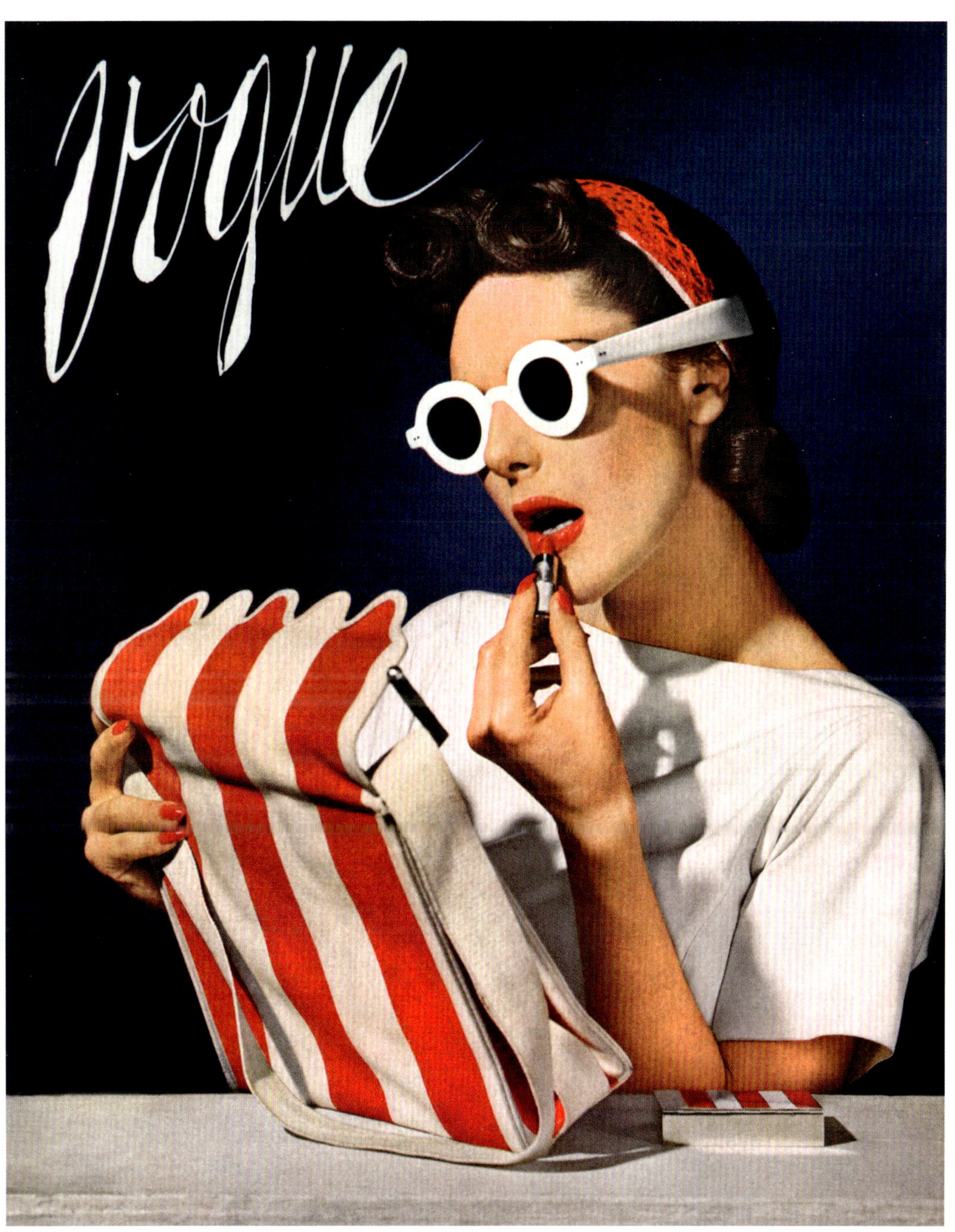

American *Vogue* cover, 1 July 1939
Muriel Maxwell, ensemble by Sally Victor, bag by Paul Flato, sunglasses by Lugene

The following works are from the V&A Collection:

Coco Chanel, Paris, 1937
V&A: E.220-2014

Estrella Boissevain, hat and coat-dress
by Bergdorf Goodman, 1938
V&A: E.221-2014

Barefoot Beauty, 1941
V&A: E.208-2014

Marquise de Montesquiou-Fezensac,
accessories by Molyneux, 1938
V&A: E.213-2014

Surreal Beauty Cream, 1941
V&A: E.212-2014

Electric Beauty, variant, 1939
V&A: E.210.2014

Electric Beauty, 1939
V&A: E.209-2014

Dress by Nettie Rosenstein,
jewellery by Trabert and Hoeffer-Mauboussin,
Tutankhamun lamp by Alberto Giacometti
V&A: E.211-2014

Miss Lane and Lisa Fonssagrives,
dresses and hats by Saks-Fifth Avenue, 1940
V&A: E.207-2014

Carmen Dell'Orefice, *Carmen Face Massage*, 1946
V&A: E.215-2014

Lisa Fonssagrives, *Hair*, 1939
V&A: E.218-2014

Lisa Fonssagrives, *Lisa with Turban*, 1940
V&A: E.206-2014

Irving Penn, New York, 1951
V&A: E.214-2014

Gloria Vanderbilt, New York, 1941
V&A: E.216-2014

Vivien Leigh, London, 1936
V&A: S.1038-2013

Noël Coward, London, 1933
V&A: S.3468-2013

New York Still Life I, 1949
V&A: E.229-2014

Persepolis Bull, 1949
V&A: E.233-2014

Pyrite, Mineral, 1946
V&A: E.223-2014

Aednium Holochrrysum, 1946
V&A: E.227-2014

Still Life, 1980s
V&A: E.230-2014

Still Life, 1980s
V&A: E.231-2014

Fashion, 1940s
V&A: E.237-2014

Dress by B.H. Wragge, hat by Sally Victor,
gloves by Wear-Right, 1948
V&A: E.235:2014